MALTA
History & Tradition

Timeline of the History of Malta

Skorba pot and human ceramic figurine

Ggantija Prehistoric Temple

St Paul's shipwreck

The Great Siege bell and Valletta

Mdina

1769	The University of Malta set up, following the expulsion of the Jesuits who had been managing the College of Studies since the end of the 16th century
1798	Grand Master Hompesch signs the capitulation of the Order to Napoleon Bonaparte
1798	The Maltese rise up in revolt against the French Republican government
1800	The French capitulate and the British take over the administration of Malta
1814	Treaty of Paris confirms Britain's possession of islands
1849	First elected members for council of government
1883	Malta Railway starts operations
1914-18	Malta becomes known as the 'Nurse of the Mediterranean' during the military and naval campaigns in the Mediterranean connected with the First World War
1919	Street riots in Valletta; four Maltese killed by British troops
1921	First Self-Government
1940	First aerial attack by Italian planes after Italy declares war against Britain and its allies
1942	Malta honoured with the granting of the George Cross by King George VI
1964	Malta gains independence from Britain, and forms part of the British Commonwealth
1974	Malta's parliament declares the establishment of the Republic of Malta
1979	Closing of last foreign military base
1989	President Mikhail Gorbachev and President George Bush meet in Malta to end the Cold War
1990	Pope John Paul II pays his first visit to Malta
2004	Malta becomes a full member of the EU

The landing of Napoleon

British coat-of-arms at the Palace, Valletta

Second World War warplaness over Malta

Declaration of Independence

St Angelo during the EU celebrations

Background image: Detail from a spiral decorated altar from Tarxien prehistoric temples.

A Historical Glimpse

In the middle of the Mediterranean Sea, where the sea narrows between the African and European continents, there is a group of strategically-situated islands. The continental shelves meet up below the sea, explaining why the area is prone to earthquakes. Just about 90 kilometres south of Sicily and about 350 kilometres north of the Libyan coast, there lies the Maltese archipelago with a surface area of about 320 square kilometres.

This group of islands is formed by Malta and Gozo, the two main inhabited islands; Comino lying in between the two main ones, with one resident family; and several other small islets, sometimes just mere rocks, around the coast. The islands are typically Mediterranean and offer little natural resources, except for the sun and the rocky inlets that have been always an attraction for seafarers. Malta, however, possesses natural deep and well-protected harbours. These were one of the island's most important assets, and that is the main reason why the different Mediterranean powers, whether for trade or for control, always desired to occupy the archipelago.

The islands are made up of sedimentary rocks which were formed around 30 million years ago when the large rivers of Europe flowed towards what today we refer to as the Mediterranean, depositing all kinds of sediment in the sea. Since the sedimentary rocks were mostly formed in the shallow waters of the sea, the islands are of marine origin. The highest point in Malta is of 253 metres, while in Gozo it is about 200 metres.

There are various places where one can appreciate the various geological formations. One of the best places is along the high cliffs of both islands, where it is possible to see the five main geological layers. These layers are Lower Coralline Limestone, Globigerina Limestone, Clays, Greensand, and Upper Coralline Limestone, at the very top. Globigerina Limestone is the main source for the building stone that has been in use throughout the human occupation of the islands. The harder Coralline Limestones are also used for some construction purposes. The clay layer has always been important, especially for agricultural purposes. That is why Gozo is greener than Malta, as the underlying layers are more clayey than Malta's. Building stone has been quarried since at least Classical times.

GOZO

COMINO

MALTA

FILFLA

Certain quarries near Għar il-Kbir have been identified as Roman. There are also certain other quarries which indicate that these would have been used for building large structures nearby. Today, because of modern machinery, quarries tend to be much deeper. The Limestone Heritage will provide the experience of visiting an authentic quarry and learn about the history of quarrying in Malta. A visit to the National Museum of Natural History, at Mdina, the Natural Sciences Museum at the Citadel in Gozo and the Limestone Heritage in Siġġiewi will help one to understand better the various natural characteristics of the islands.

The earliest traces of Man on the islands are still being debated. Recent theories suggest that the islands, which can at times be seen with the naked eye from Sicily, could have been visited by hunter-gatherers communities. Permanent settlement of the islands is given as taking place about 7,000 years ago, when the first humans settled in Malta in open-air villages, like Skorba (limits of Mġarr) and inside natural caves, like Għar Dalam (limits of Birżebbuġia). These peoples brought with them a farming mentality and various other resources that indicate a good level of organization. They introduced domesticated animals, crops, and even pottery. Their pottery indicates that these first settlers originated from south-eastern Sicily, as they brought over with them a Stentinello-type of pottery. Since that time there was a consistent settling of new people, especially from Sicily. These contacts introduced new communities, new pottery styles, as well as the occasional importation of obsidian and flint.

Although prehistoric Malta is quite rich in material remains, there is not much which dates to these early communities. Some caves have been identified as having hosted these communities, but they have not offered anything spectacular. At Skorba the remains of huts have been discovered which indicate that the first communities brought over with them knowledge making mud-bricks. Around 3500 BC, the Maltese started to erect structures which were the forerunners of the famous above-ground temples.

The origin of these temples is still open to debate. Scholars follow two lines of thoughts are suggested. They could have been developed from the rock-cut tombs that seem to pre-date the present temples or they could have been a development of the early oval huts that were introduced at Skorba. The early temples were a small affair, built with small stones, but already there was the concept of having more than one room. The early temples seem to follow a trefoil plan, which remained the basic plan of practically all the future temples that were to be built on the islands. The main differences were that there were more than just three apses, the stones became larger, and

Għar Dalam Cave, Birżebbuġa

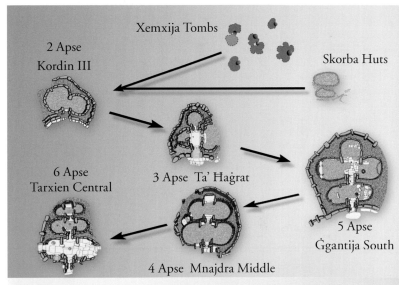

Xemxija Tombs

2 Apse
Kordin III

Skorba Huts

6 Apse
Tarxien Central

3 Apse Ta' Ħaġrat

5 Apse
Ġgantija South

4 Apse Mnajdra Middle

The suggested development of the prehistoric temples of Malta

The UNESCO World Heritage site of Mnajdra

The 'Holy of Holies' in the Hal Saflieni Hypogeum

the whole structure became even grander. The façades were architecturally conceived, which indicate that these were well planned. The internal decorations were interesting as the various decorated slabs of stones, altars, and statuary indicate.

The underground structures do not seem to have been put aside completely. Tombs have not been abundantly found, although the large complexes of the Hypogeum and the Xagħra Stone Circle indicate large necropolises catering for area communities. The recently re-discovered and excavated Xagħra Stone Circle has provided archaeologists with a lot of new material, and the artefacts discovered are still being analysed and studied. Since this complex was carved out of friable stone, it has not survived as well as the much more famous Hypogeum.

The Temple Culture came to an end around 2500 BC. A new culture arrived and introduced different customs. Cremation was introduced, while the temples that seem to have been still standing were not made use of in their entirety. Minor archaeological remains have been associated with these people, namely the dolmens, the menhirs, and the enigmatic cart-ruts. A characteristic of these people is the location of their settlements which tended to be sited on flat-topped hills,

surrounded by sheer cliffs to offer natural protection. Some of these places also had walls built on the side from where an attack was expected to come. This is the first instance of fortification walls erected in the islands. The best examples of these early fortifications are to be seen at Borġ in-Nadur, limits of Birżebbuġia, very near Għar Dalam.

The Phoenicians put the islands on the Mediterranean map. These traders of antiquity arrived in Malta to make use of its excellent harbours. They must have provided the necessary ancillary structures to make their stay even better, and they traded with the local population. Probably they ended up selling more than buying; at these early stages trade would have been conducted through bartering. Later on, coinage and writing were introduced, the latter putting Malta on the historical map. The Phoenicians seem to have settled mostly around the harbour areas, and probably made use of an existing large village roughly in the centre of Malta. Gozo could have had a similar centrally-located village. These settlements are thought to be the forerunners of present-day Mdina and Victoria in Malta and Gozo respectively.

The Phoenicians were followed by the Carthaginians, who do not seem to have introduced any great changes within

The Bronze Age site of Borġ in-Nadur with its cyclopean fortifications

Maltese society. It seems that society continued to function on much the same lines, except that now North African influences started to predominate, as can be noticed in the type of structures that have survived and in the pottery recovered.

Right: A small golden Punic amulet found at Għar il-Klieb, Rabat. Left: Punic marble cippus discovered in the 17th century.

Although the islands were attacked by the Romans during the First Punic War, it was only during the Second Punic War they occupied the islands permanently.

This was in 218 BC, and it was to initiate the long Roman occupation of the islands which lasted till about AD 400 when the islands could have been taken over by the various tribes that had invaded the Roman Empire. They subsequently fell into the Byzantine sphere of influence around 535.

Remains dated to this period are not that plentiful. Most of our knowledge has been derived from rock-cut tombs and a few buildings. The rock-cut tombs are quite numerous and their presence is usually taken to indicate a human settlement. The large concentration of tombs around Mdina and Rabat in Malta and Victoria in Gozo help us to visualize the size of these urban centres. Burial in those times had to be carried out outside the city walls, which explains their concentration immediately outside the walls. Many other tombs have been discovered in the countryside, and although not as numerous as those around the urban centres, they indicate that settlement was widespread.

The artefacts discovered in some of the tombs are quite interesting. Unfortunately many tombs had been rifled in antiquity, and therefore they can just help us to plan the settlement situation of the islands better. Otherwise they do not offer any other help in understanding this period. The material discovered consisted of pottery, coins, and jewellery. The pottery recovered includes some imported material, showing that contact with the outside world continued. There were also local imitations of foreign shapes. The coins and the other associated material help to date the tombs. There is a good numismatic collection at the Cathedral Museum at Mdina, as well as other numismatic collections which are not so readily available for public viewing. There are a few examples of local coins at the Archaeological Museum in the Citadel, in Gozo, and these indicate the type of independence that a Gozitan community enjoyed.

Gozitan coins at the Gozo Archaeological Museum

Humans have always sought to make and own jewellery. The prehistoric societies used common sea shells and bone-carved images, but the Phoenicians went a step further. They introduced glass, which became one of the materials used to make jewellery, in addition to gold and silver. There are items of jewellery like necklaces decorated with small figures, golden earrings, bracelets, and rings. Some of the buried items had been imported and buried with their owner.

Faience beads discovered in different Punic tombs

The most important event that occurred in Malta during the Roman period was the shipwreck of St Paul the Apostle. This event has also put the name of Malta in the Holy Bible, where the whole account of the shipwreck is told in the Acts of the Apostles. The coming of Paul is narrated in the fashion of

Punic pots from tombs around Mdina and Rabat

those times. Over the centuries the Maltese have created a number of stories, traditions, and folkloristic beliefs that has continued to shape the national characteristic of the Maltese.

Right: St Paul statue in Valletta by Melchiore Cafà

This event is traditionally taken to introduced Christianity into Malta, and that the Maltese have never lost their Christian religion since then. Various places are connected with this visit; some of which do make sense as Roman remains have been discovered there. Others are purely legends. This particular national and religious characteristic of the Maltese can be seen throughout the various historical eras as well as in their everyday life. Notice the various churches dedicated to St Paul, the number of street niches that are part of the street furniture, as well as the many artistic representations that have survived.

The physical remains of this period are most interesting. There are the tombs that we have already mentioned; however, during the late third century AD large complexes started to be excavated and which we now call 'catacombs'.

These were used by the various religious communities in Malta, and some of these can still be visited. The best to visit are the St Paul's and St Agatha's complexes. The latter has also a museum attached to the same site.

Palaeo-Christian oil-lamps

Besides the burial complexes, there are a few buildings dating from this period. The Domus Romana is the prime Roman site, with its various interesting artefacts as well as mosaic pavements. There is also a small collection at the Museum of Archaeology in the Citadel, Gozo. Other places are usually opened by appointment through the main offices of Heritage Malta. One of these is San Pawl Milqgħi, a place which is also traditionally connected with the shipwreck of St Paul.

The medieval period is rich in traditions, legends, and popular beliefs, but poor in material heritage. The Byzantines seem to have used the islands only sporadically, and it is possible that the islands were used as a political prison. The rising power of the Arabs and the waning of the Byzantines led to a very difficult ninth century. The Arabs conquered one city after another in North Africa. The introduction of a new religion which proclaimed respect to the people of the Book meant that resistance was not that strong by the local populations, possibly as a reaction to the rule of the Byzantines.

An Arab ceramic from the Gozo Archaeological Museum

The Maltese islands were not immediately given any due attention by the Arabs. The much larger and much richer island of Sicily was more important than the small islands lying below it. There may have been sporadic attacks on Malta, but nothing seems to have been planned before 870 when an Arab force invaded Malta from Sicily. It is not clear what exactly happened. It is said that the islands were occupied by the Arabs in 870 and they repulsed a Byzantine relief force. Others maintain that the Arabs were at first held back, but a year later that they finally took Malta. The same uncertainty is evident with regards to later events. Did the Arabs stay in Malta or did the people desert the island? Some scholars believe that the islands were left uninhabited, except for a few families making a meagre living out of the land, and they were repopulated only in the mid-eleventh century. Other historians believe that the islands remained still inhabited, albeit with a smaller population.

When, in 1091, Count Roger the Norman crossed over from Sicily to seize the Maltese islands, as he has done with most of Arab Sicily, the islands were very quickly conquered. He allowed the Arabs to stay on so long as they recognized his suzerainty and took with him the Christians who wanted to return to their homes. In 1127 his son, King Roger II [*Left; in a mosaic from Sicily*] had to return to Malta to reconquer the islands as the Arabs were becoming a little bit of a problem. The event marked the definitive re-Christianization of the islands as well as the closer contacts with Sicily and subsequently with Europe.

continues on page 12

Top: Excavations at Tas-Silġ, Marsaxlokk: this site has provided archaeologists with remains stretching from prehistory to Norman times.

Right: The remains of a Punic building at Żurrieq. The Egyptianizing cornice and perfectly fitted ashlar blocks of stone were typical of the period.

Left: One of the many tombs discovered at the Għajn Klieb necropolis, Rabat

Right: Canopied tombs at St Paul's Catacombs, Rabat.

Bottom: The Roman Baths complex, Mgarr.

Bottom right: The decorated mosaic pavement of the peristyle at the Domus Romana, Rabat.

continues from page 9

The twelfth-century tombstones [*an example below*] from the Muslim cemetery that was set up above the ruins of the Domus Romana have helped us to understand better the social structure of the period. Other material remains are, however, very scant. There are also some traces of a Norman building, maybe used as a church at the Tas-Silġ archaeological site. A medieval round tower inside Fort St Angelo may also date to this period, although there are no documents that prove the tradition that the fort was first erected by the Arabs.

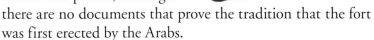

This period led to Malta having close links to Sicily. Events in Sicily would have repercussions in Malta as well. The change in the sovereigns of Sicily led to changes here as well. Whatever was introduced there ended up being adopted in Malta. Sicily and Malta passed from the Normans to the Ho-henstaufens, the Angevins, and finally the Aragonese who took control in 1282 [*Top: Escutcheons of Sicily and Aragon from Abbatija tad-Dejr catacombs, now at the Museum of Fine Arts, Valletta*]. It is even held that the famous revolt of the Sicilians, known as the Sicilian Vespers, was planned in Malta. This led to an increase of the Spanish presence in Malta and more trade options with that region. Aragonese and Catalan families came to Malta and ended up setting up their base here; today these families are part of the nobility of the islands. In Mdina, then Malta's only fortified city, a form of the local government, known as *universitas*, was established. This medieval institution had control over the day-to-day affairs of the islands, and acted in accordance with the wishes of the monarch. Its duties included that of organizing the daily coast watch by males aged between 16 and 65 years of age. They had to make sure that the fortifications of the town were up to standard. It collected and distributed accordingly taxes, either imposed from overseas or locally. They had to make sure that there was enough food in Malta and to keep with the correspondence with Sicily and even with the king wherever the court might be located at the time.

Another important institution during medieval times was the local Church. Together with the *universitas*, it managed the islands, and certain expenses were even divided between the two institutions. The main church was the Romanesque cathedral at Mdina with a single *campanile*, typical of medieval churches. Very little has survived of this building, which was rebuilt as a full-blown Baroque structure after the 1693 earthquake [*Below: A hypothetical reconstruction sketch of the old Mdina cathedral*].

There were several churches around the islands, but they were rather small in comparison to those of today. The other two most important churches were in Gozo, in the Rabat area, and in Birgu. The latter, dedicated to St Lawrence, was situated close to the medieval fortress known as the *castrum maris*. It was patronized by the local sailors as well as by the local governors and officials stationed in the castle. Several other churches were built to cater for the rural populations. Owing to the re-building programme that occurred in Malta from the mid-seventeenth century onwards, very few medieval churches have survived. One of the best examples is that of St Catherine of Alexandria at Żejtun [*below*].

Walking the winding narrow streets of Mdina [*right*] is a pleasure that gives one the right feeling of living in medieval times. Standing in front of the palaces, reading the names of the same streets, looking at the architectural styles, one gets a feeling of nobility. Other village cores, still mostly intact, can be found in the old villages. The small churches, the buildings, and the structure and feeling of these villages are typically medieval. Some later buildings have been incorporated within them but one can still feel the older spirit in these villages.

The countryside is still basically the same like as it was during the fifteenth century. The small fields, separated from one another with the typical rustic walls, the small farmhouses with their interesting architectural features, and the terracing have not changed much. Some fields tend to look abandoned, but this is not the case. Others have got typical Mediterranean small stone hut, built with dry walls. The Maltese examples are known as *girna*. In the countryside, you can notice a variety of these structures, some of which are much larger than others.

Some events of medieval times have become part of the national character and traditions. In the beginning of the fifteenth century, when the islands were still given to feudal lords, the Maltese rose up in revolt against one of these foreign nobles. The uprising was successful: although they had to pay back the money that the feudal lord had lent the Aragonese king, they were given royal assurances that the islands would not be ceded as a fief anymore. A few years later a pirate force laid siege to Mdina. The difficulty of living on such a barren island was obvious to all and that explains the small population.

With the unification of the various Spanish kingdoms, Malta became part of a world empire. In 1523 Charles V [*Below*] of Spain and Holy Roman Emperor had already been asked whether he would consider selling the islands to the homeless knights of the Order of St John. Thus began eight-year-long discussion about the future of the islands. While the knights wanted to buy the islands, Charles wanted to give the islands as a fief, against an annual payment of a falcon. Besides the islands, the knights were asked to take control of the castle of Tripoli as well. Finally in 1530 the knights accepted the donation and in October the grand master, the head of the Order of St John, arrived in Malta, giving start to the 268 years of rule by this Military and Hospitaller Order.

The Order was made up of knights from eight different regions of Europe, each representing a language of Europe: Provence, Auvergne, France, Italy, Aragon, England, Germany, and Castile. Each langue had one of its own members styled as the grand prior. The brethren voted to elect a senior knight as the overall ruler of the Order. Known as the grand master, he was elected for life. The first such grand master to rule in Malta was the Frenchman Philippe Villiers de L'Isle Adam [*Right: from St Lawrence church, Birgu*]. He had been elected in Rhodes and had participated in the siege of Rhodes that led to the Order losing its island home; he also had supervised the eight-year odyssey which ended with the arrival of the Order in Malta. After this grand master, 27 other grand masters ruled over the Order and Malta. The last one, the only German ever chosen, surrendered the islands to Napoleon Bonaparte.

The Order found around 15,000 islanders accustomed to living frugally and always in danger of raids by corsairs. This was to change dramatically. By the time the Order left Malta the population had reached 100,000, keeping in mind that during this period there were sieges, plague epidemics, and naval battles that resulted in numerous deaths. Yet, the security the knights offered, the efficient hospital system that they set up, and the jobs available to the many Maltese saw Malta experience a Golden Age.

LISLE-ADAM

continues on page 18

Left: Fort St Angelo, Vittoriosa – A castle on the site was first documented in the 13th century. The round tower is thought to date to the medieval period.

Right: A sikyfa *at the Citadel, Gozo, is one of the most important surviving Late Medieval relics.*

Far right: An Arab marble tombstone with Kufic characters, allegedly discovered in Gozo.

Left: St Agatha's cave church, Rabat – the Medieval church was decorated with murals.

Left: The old retable of the cathedral, an International Gothic work, is exhibited at the Cathedral Museum, Mdina.

Top: The coat-of-arms of the Medieval Maltese universitas, *at the Cathedral Museum, Mdina.*

Ħal Millieri church, Żurrieq: one of the few surviving medieval churches, showing the exquisite architectural features and traces of frescoes

continues from page 13

The Order did not want to settle in the old capital city, Mdina. It was too far away from the harbours, and the Order did not want to clash at such an early stage of their stay with the local nobility and Church authorities. They settled in and around the harbour area. The old castle by the sea [*Right: as it looked before 1664*] became their new headquarters and it was called Fort St Angelo. The small seaside village of Birgu became their own town. They built a line of fortifications to provide adequate defence in case of a siege. Beneath the walls of the fort and those of Birgu, they established the headquarters of their fleet. Although the main quarters of the knights were moved to the new city of Valletta in 1571, the fleet remained at Birgu throughout their stay in Malta.

A few days after the arrival of the grand master, an important public ceremony was carried out. The grand master, together with his retinue of knights and other dignitaries of

the Order, travelled to Mdina where they were greeted by the nobility and the representatives of the Maltese and the local Church, in front of the closed main entrance. The grand master vowed to respect all the laws and privileges of the Maltese people and then the main gate was opened and the grand master was feted. This was to be the first of such events, and every new grand master went to Mdina to take official possession of the city, during which ceremony the keys of the city were presented to him [*Grand Master L'Isle Adam taking possession of Mdina in a painting by Antoine de Favray found in the Grand Master's Palace, Valletta*]. In the seventeenth century, another grand master introduced the taking of the possession of Vittoriosa, and this became part of the usual ceremonies for newly-elected grand masters. In recent years these same ceremonies become part of the re-enactment activity that is annually held in Mdina or at Vittoriosa.

In 1551 a large piratical force unsuccessfully tried to attack Fort St Angelo and the harbour area. Then they moved on to Mdina where they camped in front of the old fortifications of the city for three days. Realizing that they were not strong enough to besiege the city, because of the large number of people that seemed to be there, they moved on to Gozo. After a three-day siege, they seized the island's only fortification, the ancient citadel. It is traditionally held that all of the population, about 3,000 individuals, was carried off to slavery and only very few managed to scale down the walls during the night. Only a few individuals ever made it back to Gozo.

This siege was taken to be a precursor of what was being planned on a grander scale. The knights undertook the building of new fortifications with greater earnestness. Forts St Elmo and St Michael were built in a few months and other

LA PRESA DI S. ELMO, A DI 23 GIUG.º 1565

could raise the siege kept being delayed. It only arrived in September. Since the siege was lifted on 8 September, the religious feast day that commemorates the birth of Our Lady, the grand master, the Order, the soldiers, and the Maltese attributed their deliverance to Divine help. Since then that day has become a national feast day, and a new attribution started to be attached to the titles of the Madonna, namely Our Lady of Victory.

Immediately after this long hot summer siege, the Grand Master La Valette [*Below as portrayed by d'Aleccio, fighting during the Great Siege*] wrote to his European counterparts. He thanked one and all for their praise, but he also reminded them that the Order needed material help. Financial and material help was fairly readily forthcoming. Pope Pius V immediately sent his help, including his own military architect, Francesco Laparelli da Cortona who was asked to prepare plans for the building of a new city on the

fortifications were added to the then existing line of walls; spies were sent to keep the grand master informed of the intentions of the enemy. Suleiman the Magnificent, the Ottoman sultan was nearing his end by 1565. A year before, the planning of the siege of Malta had begun. The intention was to exterminate the knights once and for all. Suleiman had been magnanimous after the defeat of the knights in 1522, but this time round he was not going to show the same generosity!

On 18 May 1565 the lookout soldiers reported the arrival of the Turkish armada. It is said that about 40,000 troops landed in Malta. There were only about 8,000 men in Malta, between knights, mercenaries, and Maltese local militia. The Ottoman troops were fortunately hindered with a divided leadership. The navy needed a safe harbour, and it was decided to start by attacking Fort St Elmo which guarded the entrance to Marsamxett Harbour. The fierce bombardments were all concentrated towards reducing Fort St Elmo to rubble. Yet, somehow the defenders resisted for a whole month [*Top: fresco at the Grand Master's Palace, Valletta by Matteo Perez d'Aleccio*], with the grand master sending fresh troops almost nightly to keep up that important resistance. When the fort fell, the Ottoman troops turned their attention towards the other fortifications on the other side of the harbour. Throughout July and August, the attacks did not stop. There were attacks on the individual forts as well as attacks on all of the fortifications. The fighting was fierce as it has been recounted in various history books. A diary kept by an Italian soldier participating in this siege has survived and was also published soon after the event. The small relief force which arrived in July was taken as a very good sign that the islands had not been abandoned to their fate. Yet, the large relief force that

L'ASSALTO ALLA POSTA DI CASTI-GLIA A DI 29 LUGLIO 1565

Valletta

The Hospital of the Order in Valletta

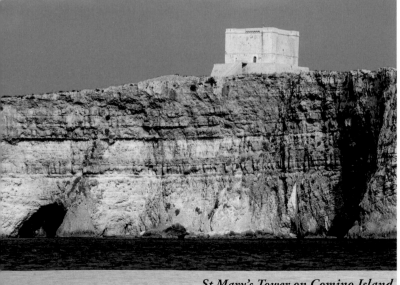

St Mary's Tower on Comino Island

peninsula that separates the Grand Harbour from Marsamxett Harbour. His plans were finally accepted, a name for the new city chosen, and on 28 March 1566 the first stone was ceremoniously laid of the new city of Valletta.

The work was frantic. No one wanted to have a fortress half-ready in case the enemy decided to return. The walls were the first to start being built. Laparelli left Malta soon after, and the supervision of the project was entrusted to the Maltese architect Girolamo Cassar. With the building of the fortifications going along fine, Cassar also planned several important buildings. The official residences of the various langues were designed by Cassar. There were also the official palaces that the Order needed for its administration, as well as the conventual church, dedicated to St John the Baptist. A hospital was also built facing the entrance to the Grand Harbour. In 1571 the headquarters of the Order was officially transferred to the new city, even though the buildings were not complete. Very quickly the city took shape.

In the euphoria after the victory over the Ottoman troops, the grand master minted some commemorative medals. One of these included the motto *Malta Renascens*, and it was quite true to say that this victory marked the rebirth of the islands. The effect of this victory was that the Order finally committed itself to stay in Malta, a decision which led to a new confidence within the Order and the local population. The rebuilding of Malta started in earnest. The sixteenth century was to see a notable demographic increase, mostly in the new city. But even the villages continued to thrive, and this meant that the countryside needed to be better protected as well.

At the beginning of the seventeenth century a process of building coastal watch towers was started at strategic coastal locations. These provided the necessary feeling and belief that Malta was safe to live in. Throughout its stay, the Order kept a process on adding to and improving the fortifications. The best foreign military architects who were brought over to Malta, advised on all the latest innovations. The seventeenth century was dominated by Italian architects, while in the eighteenth century there was an emphasis of French military strategy. The huge fortifications that were built provided the islands with a wealth that was second to none.

Walking along the bastions of Valletta is enough to get the idea of the splendour of the defence system that was employed in Valletta in the sixteenth century and added to in subsequent years. The sheer walls and bastions and the outer works are obvious examples. The cities were provided with a certain type of defence walls while the coastal defences followed various criteria. In some places a proper fort was built, while in others only small towers were built to act as a watch post. Then there was the different type of fortifications, such as batteries, redoubts, and entrenchments. As the places chosen by the military engineers were strategically sound, they were also used by the British when they took over Malta. This is also another plus point with regards to visiting Malta. Nowhere else can one see such a myriad of different fortifications built in one place, most of which can be easily visited owing to the small size of the islands.

The knights built an incredible array of buildings. They started with the plain buildings characteristic of the sixteenth century when the feeling was one of austerity as the islands were recovering from the trauma of the Great Siege. The architectural style was late Renaissance and Mannerism, which was a direct influence of the Counter Reformation tendency for austere and simple styles. The Baroque was introduced in the seventeenth century. It was first brought to the attention of the knights by that great artist, Caravaggio. A few years later Francesco Buonamici, an architect from Lucca, introduced the Baroque in architecture. From that time onwards, there was no looking back. The knights rebuilt all of their main buildings and churches. This display of power was taken on by the Maltese as well, and even the small villages started to rebuild their parish churches in the Baroque style. They soon became continuous workshops of sculpture, painting, and other interior decoration.

The Baroque treasures of Malta are too numerous to mention in a few lines. The churches of Valletta are an artistic experience in their own right. Yet, the Baroque feeling was taken outside the city and became part of Maltese culture. The main parishes were rebuilt, or had other structures added to them. The artistic treasures that can still be seen inside the churches are an affirmation of what happened in those years. One can suggest visits to the parish churches of Żejtun, Qormi, Vittoriosa, Cospicua, the two cathedrals of Mdina and Victoria in Gozo, and St George's basilica in Gozo, amongst others.

The architects who graced our islands are also interesting. Besides Francesco Laparelli who planned Valletta, others were invited over to take responsibility for the Order's building projects. At first the main architect was always a foreigner, at first Italian and then French. In the eighteenth century more local architects were given the responsibility of supervising projects. Many projects were initiated which greatly benefited the population. Early in the seventeenth century, a project to get water into Valletta was completed thanks to the building of the aqueduct, which was heavily financed by the French Grand Master Alof de Wignacourt. There was also the building of hospitals. While the one in Valletta was enlarged, other small and specialized hospitals were built in Valletta, Floriana, and Manoel Island. The latter was a quarantine hospital which was still in use in the 1960s. *continues on page 24*

Auberge of Castile

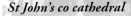

St John's co cathedral

Palazzo Spinola, St Julians

Left: The 16th-century façade of St John's co cathedral, Valletta, the work of Gerolomo Cassar.

Right: The 17th-century façade of the Mdina cathedral, the work of Lorenzo Gafà.

Top: The impressive Pinto Stores built in the 18th century and recently restored as part of the Cruise Liner Terminal.

Left: The 19th-century added façade of Siġġiewi parish church, dedicated to St Nicholas of Bari.

Top: The dining hall of Verdala Palace, with frescoes by Filippo Paladini.

Right: The gardjola, a watch tower perched on the edge of the Senglea bastions, providing a good look-out post over the Grand Harbour.

Unfortunately, there were also some difficult situations during the period. There was the 1551 landing and the Great Siege in 1565. At the end of the sixteenth century, a plague epidemic killed over 3,000 people. In 1614 there was the last major piratical landing, although this was well handled by the defenders. In 1675 another plague epidemic killed over 11,000 inhabitants out of a population of not more than 60,000. In 1693 an earthquake devastated south-eastern Sicily and also hit the Maltese islands. Although no deaths registered, immense structural damage was done. This led to a new building spree which continued unabated for many years.

The eighteenth century saw the international situation change drastically. With the French Revolution the Order lost most its independence as more and more of its territory was confiscated. The European territories of the Order had supported financially the Order's stay and its building expenses in Malta. With less income coming in, and more elderly knights deciding to retire to Malta, the financial situation became terrible. Yet, much more difficult situations were to emerge nearer the end of the century.

Napoleon Bonaparte [*Left: Napoleon's arrival to Malta*] wanted to have Malta under his control to use as a vital naval link between France and the Middle East and he planned to invade it during his Egyptian campaign. In June 1798 a large French fleet cast anchor off the islands. The French asked permission to enter the harbours to replenish the ships with water and other needs. The Order, citing international laws, said it would only allow four ships at a time to enter the harbours. This was taken as a refusal and the invasion was launched. It proved a one-sided affair, as several knights sympathized with the French general. There were also spies within the walls, besides the fact that there seems to have been a general lethargy which precluded the organization of a coordinated defence. In a few hours the Order capitulated, and Napoleon entered triumphantly into Valletta. What the French did not know was that their stay was going to be very short.

During Napoleon's six days in Malta, he issued a number of regulations which did not all go down well with the Maltese. He had promised the Maltese leaders and the Church to respect their rights, and yet he immediately went about to break these promises. On 2nd September 1798 the Maltese rose up

in revolt. This started in Rabat, and two days later Mdina was already under the control of the Maltese. This led to the Maltese blockading the French troops inside Valletta and the harbour fortifications. Help was sought from the Kingdom of the Two Sicilies, and British and Portuguese ships were sent to help. Yet, the siege would take two years of suffering on both sides of the walls, until the French capitulated and the British took over Malta.

The transition from the rule of Order to that of the French, and subsequently the British was not easy. Political realities had to be taken into consideration, as it was clear that the various European powers were realizing the strategic importance of the islands. The Treaty of Paris handed Malta over to the British, and thus started another chapter in the our history.

This was to take us into the twentieth century, during which time there were various constitutional problems, two world wars, independence, and the closure of the British bases. The islands were taken by the British because of their strategic importance. The British Fleet found the Grand Harbour and the nearby installations excellent for their needs. These continued to be added to throughout the years. The former small shipbuilding yard of the Order was enlarged and new docks built. The Grand Harbour became the home port of the British Fleet of the Mediterranean. This was the time when the harbour saw its major modern developments taking shape. New quays were built, while other harbour facilities were added. The breakwater was built at the beginning of the twentieth century and this made the harbour even safer in all kinds of weather. Malta Drydocks [*Left: the opening of the New Dock as reported in the* **Illustrated London News** *of 8 August, 1857*] became the largest employer on the islands, and this was also to be instrumental in the war effort of the British Empire throughout the two world wars.

Owing to the great facilities the British had in and around the harbour, the islands often benefited whenever the empire was involved in war. During the Greek War of Independence in the nineteenth century, the combined navies of France and Britain made use of the harbour facilities, leading to a lot of work opportunities and the realization of the need to build a new naval hospital. During the Crimean War, many allied

The recent firing of the 100-ton RML gun at Rinella Battery, a 19th-century British coastal fortification

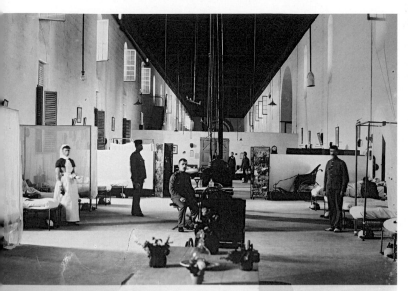

The Great Hall of the Order's Hospital re-utilized in World War One

Aeroplanes in Maltese skies during the Second World War

Fort Manoel under aerial attack during the Second World War

troops passed through Malta which proved a good staging depot for the advance to the east. During the First World War Malta was nicknamed 'the Nurse of the Mediterranean', for the hospital services it provided to the allied troops who were in need of medication and recuperation after the various battles in the Eastern Mediterranean. The Second World War was to be a completely different thing.

By now aeroplanes had been introduced into battle as an essential part of the war scenario. Air attacks became possible, and the islands were not spared. The day after the declaration of war on Britain and its allies by Italy under the Fascist dictator Mussolini, the islands were attacked. Thus started in 1940 the Second Great Siege of Malta and lasted up to 1943 when the Italian navy surrendered in the harbours of Malta. Ironically this surrender occurred on 8 September, as had happened during the Great Siege of 1565. Once more the Maltese saw that this as a sign of timely divine intervention. The war caused a lot of suffering and material destruction throughout the islands, especially in and around the Grand Harbour area.

Many people moved out of these dangerous places. Others turned once more to what nature has provided the islands with, the local stone. They dug rock-cut shelters into the ditches of the various bastions of the knights. Shelters were dug in various places, some of which have been recently cleaned and opened to the general public. Whole families lived and survived throughout the whole period of the war in these shelters. The destruction of homes led to a movement of people never witnessed before in Malta. Rural villages became overcrowded with refugees who had either lost their home or else did not want to live in constant danger.

The defence of the islands was carried out by the air force which prevented enemy bombers from reaching Malta; the artillery, who tried to keep the enemy as far away from its targets as possible; and the navy who made every effort to transport food and other needs to the beleaguered islands, through a dangerous Mediterranean Sea. In 1942 Malta and its people were awarded the George Cross by King George VI as an official recognition of the island's courage. This honour has also been officially recognized by subsequent Maltese governments and the George Cross is part of the national flag. Also in 1942 a bomb pierced the Mosta dome but failed to explode; none of the more than 300 people were injured. That too was taken to be a miracle.

Notwithstanding the official recognition of Malta's importance, the situation was becoming more difficult. There was a general lack of food, while the armed forces had little supplies left. Fuel and ammunition were so scarce that ammunition was rationed. There was even talk of an imminent surrender. In London plans were made to send some supplies to see the islands manage for another three months, if the convoy got through. On the days before 15 August, another important religious feast day, ships started to get through. Although many ships had been sunk during the voyage from Gibraltar to Malta, five got through. This convoy, officially known as Operation Pedestal, was soon renamed the Santa Maria Convoy, and once more the Maltese population believed that Divine intervention had managed to get this precious little help. This was the turn of the war for Malta. Subsequently more convoys entered the harbour, with more supplies of food and ammunition. A year later the islands were used to invade Sicily, thus completely reversing the roles with the islands now being used as a base to attack Sicily.

Provision arrives in the Grand Harbour during Second World War

The aftermath of the Second World War was a challenge to one and all. The political situation had changed drastically. The Maltese were asking for more representational government and a much more liberal constitution. There was also the rebuilding programme caused by the enormous damage of the aerial bombardments. Meanwhile Britain was already planning to downsize its overseas bases, which would affect drastically the local economy. The various Maltese governments started to work on the industrialization of the island, as well as giving more importance to the new tourism industry. The political work was to lead to the granting of independence from Britain on 21 September 1964. The British bases remained in Malta, as this was still the period of the Cold War, and the islands aerial, military and naval facilities were considered as very important. On 13 December 1974 Malta was declared a republic within the Commonwealth, thus retaining the connection with Britain. Five years later, on 31 March 1979, there was the final closure of the British base in Malta. For the very first time, no foreign troops were stationed on the islands.

The declaration of the Republic of Malta on 13 December 1974

Malta is a member of many international fora, including the United Nations and the Commonwealth. In May 2004 it joined the European Union. In recent years, several important personalities have visited Malta. In 1989 it was the turn of the American President George Bush and the Soviet leader Mikhail Gorbachev. In their talks, they agreed to dismantle the old post-Second World political system, marking the official end of the Cold War. In 1990 and 2001 Pope John Paul II visited Malta; the second time he beatified two local religious and one local priest. In November 2005 the Commonwealth biennial conference was held in Malta. The visiting dignitaries included almost all the heads of state of the Commonwealth countries and Queen Elizabeth II.

Illuminations welcoming Malta's entry into the EU in 2004

Valletta and Floriana

When the knights of St John arrived in Malta in 1530, the peninsula on which Valletta and Floriana were to be built was practically uninhabited. There was a small church and probably a tower at its tip, to watch over the entrance to the harbours and perhaps a few farmhouses. The area was immediately recognized by the knights as an excellent strategic site for a fortified city. This was a constant thought in the minds of the grand masters, the knights, and the military engineers who were brought over to Malta during the first thirty years of the Order's stay.

The very first structure to be built was Fort St Elmo. The piratical attack of 1551 made it clear to the knights that they were in grave danger. There were no adequate defences and they decided to build fortifications in case that raid was just a spying mission. A year later a small star-shaped fort was erected to the designs of Pietro Pardo. It was built in such a hurry that it was said that attackers would take it in a few days. Because of this detail, various grand masters continued to add walls and better fortifications, without actually making it better. Other suggestions and even plans were prepared to build a fortified city but, since it was felt that an attack was imminent and there was not enough money to start such a large project, they were postponed. In 1565, when a large Ottoman armada landed in Malta, only Fort St Elmo was in place.

The Great Siege was fought around the Grand Harbour area. Before the loss of Fort St Elmo, the Ottomans used the high ground of the promontory to attack both the fort and the other side of the harbour fortifications. The successful end of the siege in September of the same year, led to the knights to insist with the European powers that both material and financial help was needed quickly, or else they would abandon the islands. Help thus was sent, which included Francesco Laparelli, the pope's military architect.

Laparelli immediately went about working out a feasible plan and, on 28 March 1566, the first stone of the new city was laid. The line of fortifications was quickly erected and soon the first buildings rose behind them. Amongst the first to be buried inside the church of Our Lady of Victories was Grand Master Jean de Valette [*above; his coat of arms*], the hero of the Great Siege, who had insisted on this new city. The definite transfer of the headquarters of the Order from Vittoriosa to Valletta in 1571 led to a series of building programmes, which was to become an ongoing exercise. The first buildings were erected in the style of the time, namely late Renaissance and Mannerism. In the seventeenth century Baroque was introduced and this led to more buildings, and sometimes the pulling down of others in order to rebuild them in the new style. Various architects were brought over to continue with this trend and painters were also invited to decorate the interior of the churches and palaces.

The fortifications of Valletta on the Marsamxett harbour side

An 18th-century painting showing the fortifications protecting Valletta

In the 1630s, during another invasion scare, the Order brought over Pietro Paolo Floriani, a military architect, who suggested the building of a front line of fortifications to defend better the landward defences of Valletta. Although work started, there was some opposition to these fortifications and they were not completed then. These fortifications, which came to be known as the Floriana Lines, were completed during the eighteenth century. Originally it was not meant to have any urban buildings behind the lines of Floriana, but gradually certain buildings started to rise. In the first half of the eighteenth century, during the magistracy of Grand Master Anton Manoel de Vilhena, permission was given for houses to be built, and the suburb of Floriana was born and officially called *Subborgo Vilhena*. The Maltese, however, gave it the name of Floriana and that name has stuck.

Valletta became the capital city of the islands. Buildings were erected for the various offices necessary at the time. Most of these buildings are still in use, sometimes for the same function as they had been originally planned for. Churches were also constructed, because the Order was a religious one, besides the fact that religious Orders were given land to build their own convents and churches. Although Floriana holds some interesting buildings, these were usually built after space ran out in Valletta.

The entrance to Valletta lies through the fortifications of Floriana. The main entrance was, and still is, Portes des Bombes, which looks like a double triumphal arch although originally it was just a plain entrance into the city of Valletta. The decorated stonework recalls the Baroque mentality of the time. In the nineteenth century, as traffic was increasing, the British added another entrance; while the fortifications on either side were later pulled down to facilitate access into Valletta.

Floriana boasts of a few but highly interesting churches. The parish church is dedicated to St Publius, traditionally held to be the first bishop of Malta. Its feast day usually opens up the summer festive season. This church fronts one of the widest open areas in Malta which is known as 'the granaries'. Built by the British on the same lines as those built by the knights, the granaries were storage vats for grain. They were still in use till a few years back. Just behind this church, there is the seventeenth-century round church dedicated to the Immaculate Conception, better known as the church of Sarria. Originally there was a small church built by an Italian knight with the surname of Sarria. The present edifice was erected in lieu of a votive offering by the Order during the plague of 1675–76. It was designed by Mattia Preti and the paintings inside are by this Italian artist and by his *bottega*. Close by there are the Malta Diocese offices, known as the Curia. This is an interesting eighteenth-century building which was originally built as a retreat house.

Right: Portes des Bombes was originally a one-gate entrance into Floriana. A second gate was added in the 19th century, and in the 1950s the adjacent fortifications were pulled down to help in the better flow of traffic.

The Police Headquarters across the street used to be an old people's home built in the eighteenth century.

Another church and convent belongs to the Capuchin friars. Built on the highest fortifications of the suburb, this church and convent were destroyed during the Second World War but rebuilt immediately afterwards. The friars have preserved many of the old paintings, as well as the unique and interesting crypt, which is definitely worth a visit.

Floriana is also known for its many gardens. There are several gardens on the fortifications that surround the suburb. They provide excellent views of the harbours and also contain monuments commemorating different events and personalities. Another garden, the Mall, was erected so that the knights could play the game of Pall Mall. Several monuments commemorating important recent personalities can be seen there. Entering Valletta through the main City Gate, one is greeted by massive fortifications meant to deter the enemy. The walls were excavated from the living rock, and the wide and deep ditch was meant to be the main deterrent. The bridge was narrower and the last part, made out of wood, was drawn at sunset.

Valletta was planned on a grid-iron design with straight streets and others intersecting the main ones. The main street leads straight down to Fort St Elmo. The three main streets of Valletta are the widest ones, while the others are much narrower. Open squares were planned to provide

areas where soldiers could gather in case of an attack and also spaces for ceremonies and pageants to be held and crowds to gather.

The palace of the grand master is one of the main buildings of Valletta. It was the official residence of the grand master, as well as the place where the Council and all the other official ceremonies were held. The British used the palace as the official residence and office of the governor; today it houses the Maltese parliament as well as being the official office of the president of the Republic. Some state rooms are open to the public and these offer a chance to see how the knights had decorated these halls. There are frescoes depicting the story of the Order before it arrived in Malta and the main events of the Great Siege. The Tapestry Chamber is decorated with a unique set of Gobelins tapestries. These were commissioned specifically for this particular hall, and they were a gift of Grand Master Perellos. The famous Palace Armoury is housed in the former stables of the palace. The Armoury, which boasts of a good number of suits of armours from the sixteenth, seventeenth, and eighteenth centuries, is managed by Heritage Malta.

The knights were organized into eight different Languages. Each language had its own hostel or auberge as they are known in Malta. Of the eight auberges built in Valletta,

continues on page 38

Left: Auberge of Provence, presently the National Museum of Archaeology, Valletta.

Right: Piazza Regina; one of the squares in Valletta with their popular open air cafes.

Top: The star-shaped Fort St Elmo, built in 1552 to provide defence to the Valletta harbours.

Left: Façade of Auberge of Castile, an 18th-century baroque palace designed by Andrea Belli.

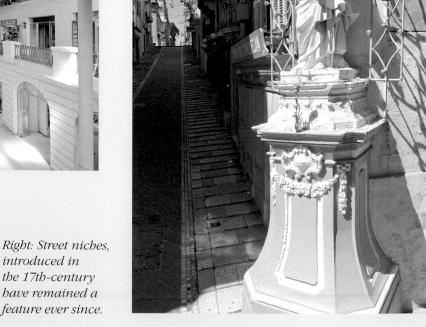

Top: The Valletta market, built in 1859, is a combination of Malta stone and cast iron framework.

Right: Street niches, introduced in the 17th-century have remained a feature ever since.

Right: The large decorated main hall of the Auberge of Provence, set up for a contemporary exhibition.

Left: The Manoel Theatre, the first purposely-built theatre in Malta.

Left: The vault of St John's co cathedral, a baroque masterpiece decorated by Mattia Preti.

Right: The council chamber with the unique complete set of Gobelins tapestries.

Top: The Palace Armoury, with a display of arms and armour from the 16th to the 18th century.

Left: The Beheading of St John, *a masterpiece by Caravaggio in the oratory at St John's co cathedral.*

Bottom: Sculptured stone altars from the prehistoric temples of Tarxien, at the National Museum of Archaeology.

Left: Well-balanced features looking onto the internal yard of Auberge of Castile, the present office of the Prime Minister.

Top: Valletta harbour, during a lull from its commercial activity, with local fishermen enjoying the day.

Top: The firing of the gun, held daily at noon at the Upper Barrakka saluting battery.

Right: The lower hall of the Hospital of the Order, with its impressive ribbed vaulting.

The main hall of the Auberge of Castile

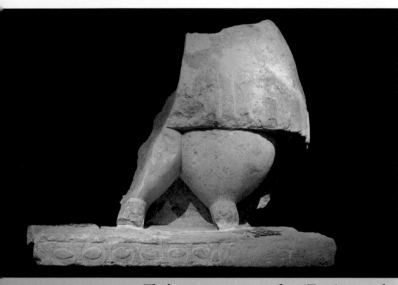

The largest stone statue from Tarxien temples

The marble decorated cartouche on the façade of the Auberge of Italy

continues from page 31

only five have survived. The most impressive is that of Castile, which houses the office of the prime minister. Originally designed by Gerolamo Cassar in the sixteenth century, it was rebuilt completely in the eighteenth century to the designs of Andrea Belli. The facade is magnificently Baroque. The stairs that lead up to the main entrance, the main portal with its stone columns, the decorated entablature with the bust of Grand Master Pinto surrounded by a trophy of arms, the floral decorations around the central window, and the coat-of-arms of the same grand master, together with the coat-of-arms of the language that occupied this palace, are part and parcel of a whole theatrical statement.

Another interesting building is the auberge of Provence in Republic Street. Also designed by Cassar, the edifice was added to during the late seventeenth and early eighteenth centuries. The place was used as a small guest house in the nineteenth century, and then turned into a private social club. Since the 1950s it has housed first the National Museum and now the National Museum of Archaeology. This museum boasts of several important prehistoric items, like the original stonework from the Tarxien temples, the Sleeping Lady, the Venus of Malta, and many other unique artefacts.

The Italian knights built their auberge in Merchants Street. The façade was given its present appearance during the reign of Grand Master Carafa. The *cartouche* over the main entrance is a work of art in Baroque theatricality. The English knights never managed to build their own auberge as, by the time Valletta was built, there were no more English knights. When, in the eighteenth century, the Bavarians wanted to have their own auberge different from the German one, they were attached to the dormant English *langue*. The palace – the Auberge of Baviere – that was occupied by them is still standing. The last auberge that is still standing is the one that belonged to the knights from Aragon, Catalonia, and Navarre. This is one of the jewels of sixteenth-century architecture. It was planned by Gerolamo Cassar, and, fortunately, unlike his other auberges, it was never touched or rebuilt and provides us with a good idea of how the first buildings in Valletta looked like.

There were built many other palaces built by knights and other individuals. Although the knights had to participate in the various activities held by their own langue, in actual fact some of them were so rich and powerful that they built their own palaces. Grand Commander Verdelin built his own town house opposite the palace of the grand master. It is still standing and it is easy to understand why such a building would have attracted the attention and admiration of onlookers. Its balconies faced the main square, and they are still considered amongst the best-placed balconies in Valletta. The palace is also one of the first Baroque buildings in Valletta, and is attributed to Francesco Buonamici,

The building which houses the National Museum of Fine Arts is considered as one of the most prestigious in the city. Although there had been other buildings on the site, the present edifice was constructed in the eighteenth century to entice one of the richest knights to retire there. The architect may have been Andrea Belli, because of its magnificent stairway which is considered as one of the loveliest stairways in Malta. The paintings it houses date from the fourteenth century down to modern times. There are works by Mattia Preti, Matthias Stomer, Antoine de Favray, and many other foreign artists. Maltese talent is represented by Francesco Zahra, Stefano Erardi, Giuseppe Calì, and others. Antonio Sciortino's sculptures are well known from the various monuments that can be admired in the streets and squares of Valletta and Floriana. The museum houses an excellent collection of plaster casts of some of his monuments, as well as the original bronze work of *Les Gavroches*, or the Street Urchins of Paris.

The Bibliotheca was the last public building the Order erected in Valletta. Designed by Stefano Ittar, it was planned to house the archives and the massive book collections of the Order. It is still used as a Bibliotheca and houses the archives of the Order. This is the place to carry out research about the Order and the islands during that time and to research about the nineteenth and twentieth centuries by reading through the newspapers published in Malta. One needs to show some kind of identification to visit the Bibliotheca.

The various large buildings of Valletta are mostly to be found along the main streets. The large Palazzo Francia Buttigieg, the first large building as soon as one enters the city, was built in the nineteenth century and was meant to show a move away from the Baroque style that had dominated the islands since the seventeenth century. The building was well complemented with the erection of the Royal Opera House, on the opposite side of the street. The Opera House had a very tragic history. There were problems with the plans, owing to the fact that the English architect had never been to Malta before he planned the theatre. Then its interior of the building was gutted by fire. Lastly, it was hit by a number of bombs during the Second World War, and it has remained in ruins ever since.

This was not the first theatre in Valletta; the Manoel Theatre had been inaugurated in 1732. Designed by Romano Carapecchia, the theatre was a gift from Grand Master Anton Manoel de Vilhena. It was Malta's first custom-built place for theatrical productions. Before, such presentations were held in the main halls of the large palaces. With the inauguration of the theatre, the local population soon became enamoured of it.

The 16th-century Auberge of Aragon, planned by Gerolomo Cassar

The main staircase of the National Museum of Fine Arts

The Reading Room of the National Library

The Manoel Theatre

Modern artistic expressions at St James Cavalier

The Long Hall of the Holy Infirmary, the hospital of the Order

Although this theatre actually had lost much of its importance during the lifespan of the Royal Opera House, it regained its importance after the Second World War. Today, the Manoel Theatre is the main cultural centre of the islands. It has a small interesting museum and the actual theatre is being restored.

The other theatres in Valletta are not as historically important as the Manoel Theatre. The fortress-like tower, St James Cavalier, has been rehabilitated as a cultural centre for creativity. It is used for the holding of exhibitions, music concerts, and small theatrical productions. Another place which offers the same kind of facilities but on a bigger scale is the Mediterranean Conference Centre. The building was originally constructed as the Sacra Infermeria, or the Holy Infirmary of the Order. Within its halls, the knights provided the necessary medical help to one and all. They used to serve their patients on silver plates, and it was also obligatory for the grand master to go and help out in the hospital at least once a week. Attached to this hospital there were other smaller sections which catered for different illnesses and medical needs. A school of anatomy was also set up here. During the Second World War it suffered structural damage and it was only in the late 1970s that it was restored to function as a Conference Centre.

Near this centre, there is Fort St Elmo, the first building to be erected on the peninsula. This fort saw action during the Great Siege and, although it was won by the Ottoman troops, it survived for a whole month, and this was beneficial to boost the morale of the Christian troops. Soon after the enemy troops left in September, the rebuilding started, and this fort retained its importance throughout the knights' stay. It was enlarged and encircled with more walls to make it more difficult to take. The arrival of the British saw the fort change hands, although not its importance in the overall defence of the Grand Harbour. It was still a military place till the 1970s. Today, part of the fort is used as a police academy and the other part is being restored. There is also the highly-interesting National War Museum.

The museum lies within a nineteenth-century drill hall. There are a good number of war relics dating to the British period in Malta. Although the whole 180 years or so are remembered, the emphasis is on the activities and events connected with the Second World War, when the islands became a prime target for the Axis aerial attacks. The main exhibits are part of the Gloster Gladiator, one of three such planes that provided the first aerial defence to the islands; some guns which proved so important in the defence of Malta; and a lot of photographs of the main events and personalities connected with the war.

To appreciate Valletta, one has to walk around the streets and the bastions, and to admire all the views that these offer. The bastions are in fact part of the heart of Valletta. The walks along the bastions offer different views of Marsamxett and the Grand Harbour. In three places gardens have been laid out on these bastions. Today they have been rehabilitated and they are quite important relaxing oases for visitors. The most important of these is the Upper Barracca Gardens. Situated at the highest point of the fortifications facing the Grand Harbour, it dominates the harbour, the rest of Valletta, as well as the landward fortifications towards Floriana. From here, one can very easily admire the fortifications and the way that they were built. One can admire excellently the fortifications' depth and how difficult it was for the enemy to make an entry from this side.

The gardens are also interesting because they offer an excellent view of the Grand Harbour. This can be truly said to be one of the most impressive harbour views anywhere in the Mediterranean. One can appreciate the fortifications of Fort St Angelo and the Three Cities, namely Vittoriosa, Senglea, and Cospicua. Just beneath the balcony, there is the saluting battery which has been restored and some nineteenth-century guns placed here. A heritage society interested in military fortifications organizes tours and even a re-enactment of the firing of the guns every day at noon. These gardens are also a small gallery of monuments, some of which are notable works of art. There is the last resting place of the British Governor Maitland. There is a monument to Lord Strickland, one of Malta's prime ministers, by Antonio Sciortino, to Giuseppe Calì, one of the most prolific painters of the nineteenth and twentieth centuries, and to Winston Churchill.

From the balcony, one can see that there is another garden, situated farther down the hill, closer to the entrance of the Grand Harbour. This is known as the Lower Barracca Gardens. It is smaller in size and only has a couple of monuments. The older one is an interesting piece of architecture. Built early in the nineteenth century, it commemorates one of the best-loved British officials that had helped the Maltese insurgents against the French, Sir Alexander Ball. The monument was built in the form of a Greek temple, and it has been restored more than once. It dominates the area, with its columns, statues, and size. From this garden one can have a good look across the first part of the Grand Harbour, Rinella Creek, Fort Ricasoli, as well as the monument that was erected to commemorate the heroes who died on the seas during the Second World War. The monument is in the form of a round bell tower, and its bell is rung at noon every day.

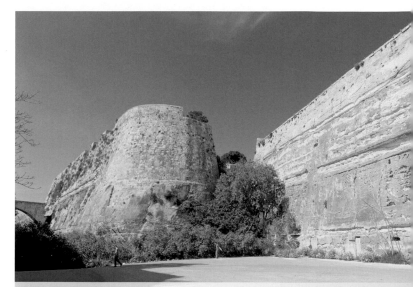

The main ditch and fortifications of Valletta

The Upper Barrakka Gardens

The Lower Barrakka Gardens

The Siege Bell – commemorating the dead of World War Two

The church of St Paul Shipwrecked on the feast day

The third garden on the bastions of Valletta is known as Hastings Garden. Till the beginning of the nineteenth century, there were no plants or trees planted here. After the burial of the Marquis of Hastings, one of the first British governors in Malta, the local people started bringing flowers on his tomb, and finally a proper monument was erected and a small garden created around it. The garden offers good views of the surrounding fortifications, the suburb of Floriana, and Marsamxett Harbour.

From the different views that these gardens offer of the skyline of Valletta, it is also possible to note that various domes, spires, and other ecclesiastical buildings abound. The city having been built by a Religious Order, the knights invited and offered land to various other Religious Orders, who subsequently settled in Valletta. These churches were added throughout the years to satisfy different needs or as votive offerings. Other churches were built after the arrival of the British.

The most important church in Valletta is the co-cathedral of St John. The former conventual church of the Order, this is also one of the biggest tourist attractions in Malta. It is a sixteenth-century building with a seventeenth- and eighteenth-century interior. Designed by Gerolamo Cassar, it was used by all the different languages of the Order. With the introduction of the Baroque style, the interior started to be transformed by Mattia Preti, the Italian artist who settled in Malta in 1661. The nave is considered as one of his masterpieces. The church has a magnificent floor covered by about 400 multi-coloured tombstones, reminding us of the various personalities that were in Malta during that time, and ended buried, or commemorated, with these works of art. There are the monuments mostly commemorating the various grand masters of the Order who ruled Malta. There are also side altars with many important canvases. The most famous of them all is that by Caravaggio, which is to be found in the Oratory. The Beheading of St John the Baptist is one of the greatest masterpieces of the early Baroque. Attached to the church there is a museum which is worth a visit, as there are more artistic treasures. There are the seventeenth-century reliquary that used to hold the relic of the hand of St John the Baptist (a gift of Grand Master Carafa), the Flemish tapestries (a gift from Grand Master Perellos), a number of church vestments (gifts from different members of the Order), choral books, and many other important artistic artefacts.

The other churches in Valletta are important for various reasons. The city's three parishes, cater for the spiritual needs of the local population. They are dedicated to Our Lady of Safe Haven, St Paul Shipwrecked, and St Augustine respectively. The churches were first built in the sixteenth century but, like many other buildings in Valletta, they passed through many extensions, rebuilding, and additions to the original fabric. The church dedicated to St Paul Shipwrecked has many artistic treasures. The canvases are of high standard, especially the sixteenth-century main altarpiece, while the processional statue is considered as one of the best such statues in Malta. It is the work of the seventeenth-century Maltese sculptor Melchiorre Gafà (Caffa or even Cafà) who studied and worked in Rome. Considered a worthy rival to the great Bernini, he unfortunately died at a young age. During the week leading up to 10 February, the church is bedecked in all its finery and all its most important treasures. That day is one of the public holidays of Malta.

Various other churches in Valletta were originally built by the knights. The first building erected in Valletta is thought to have been a small church, dedicated to Our Lady of Victory. It was commissioned by himself, and it was his own private church. Here he was also the first to be buried before his mortal remains were transferred to the crypt of St John's church after its completion. Facing it is the church dedicated to St Catherine of Alexandria, a sixteenth-century structure which was enlarged and beautified by Romano Carapecchia, one of the Italian artists who was a great promoter of Roman Baroque.

The churches of Valletta reflect different aspects about history, art, and religious experiences. The parishes all organize their annual feast days, with band marches and a procession with the titular statue. Besides that, there are a small number of other annual votive processions. The Good Friday procession comes out from the church dedicated to St Mary of Jesus, run by the Franciscan Minors. It is a solemn procession that commemorates the Passion of Jesus Christ in eight statuary groups. Inside the church there is also an impressive seventeenth-century Crucifix. It is held to be a miraculous image and the devotion of the people towards it is quite evident.

During the time of the knights, there was a small Greek community in Malta, living mostly in Valletta. The small church was built to cater for their spiritual needs was destroyed during the Second World War, but has since been rebuilt. Its two main icons are greatly venerated by the faithful and appreciated by art lovers. The most important is the large icon of Our Lady of Damascus.

In the nineteenth century, the British felt the need to build churches for their own. The first that was built was St Paul's cathedral which introduced the style of Neo-Classical architecture and ended up dominating the skyline of Valletta with its long spire. It had been originally planned by a British architect, whose plan failed due to his lack of knowledge regarding the local stone. A resident British architect amended the plans, and completed the building of the Cathedral.

St Andrews Scots church was built during the second half of the nineteenth century. Planned by a Maltese architect, this church reflects the mentality of the time with regards to architecture, but at the same time it does not look too much of an intrusion on Valletta's skyline. Both of these churches are still in use by the resident British community.

Valletta churches and buildings at twilight

A detail of the façade of the Dominican church

Walking the streets of Valletta is always a pleasure. One can find so many different details on the facades of the buildings, the street niches, the monuments, and the squares that come up without any warning. The streets of Valletta are busy in the morning but they seem to calm down later on in the afternoon when the tourists and the Maltese shoppers return to their hotels or homes. The main streets are interesting, but there is also a lot to see and to discover in the other areas. This is a small city and therefore it is highly recommended that one tries to discover as much of the history and feeling of Valletta as possible. No wonder that the capital city of Malta has been declared a UNESCO World Heritage Site.

Left: A re-enactment of the Kukkanja, *a carnival activity introduced in 1723.*

Right: The closed wooden balconies, an important feature of many Valletta houses.

Top: Fresh fruit and vegetables from the greengrocer in a side street in Valletta.

Left: Teenagers chatting in the shade, in Valletta.

Top: Faith one of the three biplanes that defended Malta during the beginning of the Second World War seen at the War Museum in Fort St Elmo, Valletta.

Right: A baroque concert in the Presidential Palace corridors.

Valletta and its harbours and fortifications

Pieta Creek

CRAIG
LORENZ
ZAMMIT
CLAPP
BORTON

St Lukes Hospital

22

6   TRIQ NAZZJONALI

TRIQ L-INDIPENDENZA

RMF

Porte des Bombes

Crown Works

St Francis Ravelin

(HORNS DITCH)
(FOSS KORNI)

SPCA

TRIQ IL- BELT MAZNA

LICENSING & TESTING

Braxia Cem.

Jubilee Grove

Gozo Ferry
Boat House
TRIQ W. BONNICI
Gozo Channel HQ

Bocci
Sa' Maison

TRIQ SA' MAISON

Notre Dame Ravelin

POLICE GARAGE

IL - FOSSTA NOTRE DAME

Argotti Botanical Gardens

St Phillip

Magazine Bastion

Cappuchin Curtain

Hay Wharf

Gardens

Salvatore Bastion

Polversita Bastion

Ozpizio

Trade Sch

LOTTO

Immigration
POLICE HQ

PJAZZA SAN KALCIDONJU

Curia

TRIQ L-ILJUN (LION ST)

V. BUGEJA
V. DIMECH
ARGOTTI
KONSERV

IL - MALL

Maglio Gardens

TRIQ SARRIA

The Granaries

TRIQ SAN PUBLJU
ISQOF M. CARUANA
SAN TUMAS
TRIQ SAN MIRA TUR

LOPEZ

Msida Bastion

Library

GOVT OFFICES

Bocci

Independence Monument

IR-RE DWARDU VII

P

6

War Monument

Excelsior

HANNIBAL SCICLUNA

L-ASSEDJU L-KBIR (GREAT SIEGE RD)

St John Counterguard

TRIQ L-ASSEDJU

Phoenicia

Triton Fountain

Main Bus Terminus

St John Bastion
St John Cavalier

St James Bastion

St James Counterguard

St James Cavalier

H. Ganado Gdns

TRIQ GIROLAMO CASSAR

St James Counterguard

SQAQ HARPUR

IT-TELGHA TA' KURCIFISS

(CRUCIFIX HILL)

Borza ta' Malta

National Museum of Fine Arts

H

St Michaels Bastion

St Andrews Bastion

Hastings Gdn.

INGIERI
L-IMTIEHEN
VASSALLI

SANT ANDRIJA
SAN BIAGJU

TRIQ L-ORDINANZA

TRIQ MELITA

TRIQ IL-PAPA PIJU V

South St

Freedom Sq.

TRIQ NOFS IN - NHAR

TRIQ IZ- ZAKKARIJA

Castille

BATTERIJA

Upper Barakka Gardens

SAN ANTON

War Rooms

TRIQ IR- R

TRIQ MELITA

GNIEN IS-SULTAN

Fort Lascaris

IX-XATT TA' LASCARIS

Customs

International Sea Ferry Terminal

IX-XATT TA'KURCIFISS
IX-XATT TA'KURCIFISS

TRIQ PINTO

Valletta Waterfront

Crucifix Wharf

Lascaris Wharf

H

National Museum of Archaeology

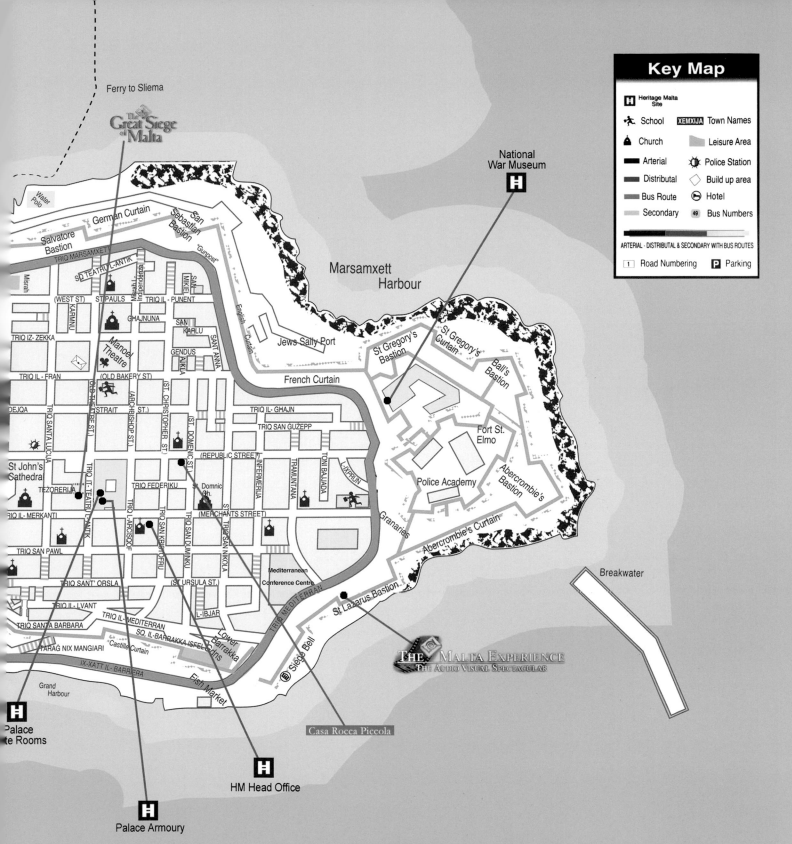

Key Map

H Heritage Malta Site	
🏃 School	**XEMXIJA** Town Names
⚓ Church	Leisure Area
▬ Arterial	☀ Police Station
▬ Distributal	◇ Build up area
▬ Bus Route	Ⓗ Hotel
Secondary	**49** Bus Numbers

ARTERIAL - DISTRIBUTAL & SECONDARY WITH BUS ROUTES

| **1** Road Numbering | **P** Parking |

Ferry to Sliema

The Great Siege of Malta

Water Polo

German Curtain

San Sebastian Bastion "Gunpost"

Salvatore Bastion

TRIQ MARSAMXETT

SD TEATRU IL-ANTIK

Misrah

(WEST ST) KARMNU

ST PAULS

Misrah L-Independenza

TRIQ IL - PUNENT

SAN MIKIEL

SAN ANNA

Marsamxett Harbour

National War Museum **H**

TRIQ IZ- ZEKKA

GHAJNUNA

SAN KIARLU

GENDUS

AIKLA

Manoel Theatre

(OLD BAKERY ST)

Jews Sally Port

St Gregory's Bastion

St Gregory's Curtain

Ball's Bastion

TRIQ IL - FRAN

(ARCHBISHOP ST)

(OLD THEATRE ST) STRAIT

(ST. CHRISTOPHER ST)

(ST. DOMENIC ST)

French Curtain

DEJQA

TRIQ SANTA LUCIJA

(REPUBLIC STREET)

TRIQ IL- GHAJN

TRIQ SAN GUZEPP

INFERMERIJA

TRAMUNTANA

TONI BAJJADA

L-IKPRUN

Fort St. Elmo

St John's Cathedral

TEZORERIJA

TRIQ IL-TEATRU L-ANTIK

TRIQ FEDERIKU

St Domnic Ch.

Police Academy

Abercrombie's Bastion

TRIQ IL - MERKANTI

TRIQ L-ARCISQOF

TRIQ SAN KRISTOFRU

(MERCHANTS STREET)

TRIQ SAN DUMINKU

TRIQ SAN NIKOLA

Granaries

Abercrombie's Curtain

TRIQ SAN PAWL

(ST URSULA ST.)

Mediterranean Conference Centre

TRIQ SANT' ORSLA

TRIQ IL - LVANT

SQ. IL-BARRAKKA ISFEL Gdns

Lower Barrakka Gdns

L-IBJAR

TRIQ MEDITERRAN

St Lazarus Bastion

Breakwater

TRIQ SANTA BARBARA

TRIQ IL - MEDITERRAN

"Castille Curtain"

TARAG NIX MANGIARI

Siege Bell

THE MALTA EXPERIENCE
THE AUDIO VISUAL SPECTACULAR

IX-XATT IL- BARRERA

Fish Market

Grand Harbour

H Palace State Rooms

Casa Rocca Piccola

H HM Head Office

H Palace Armoury

VALLETTA

49

Carnival

Once a year Carnival is celebrated in various localities around the islands. The main carnival competition, which includes children's carnival, dance routine, and carnival floats of different sizes, is held in Valletta. Several villages have taken up the tradition to organize their own, and some of which are quite interesting. Carnival was always connected with religion, although nowadays the only religious thing that has survived is that it is held according to the Roman Catholic Church calendar. Otherwise, the noise, the colours, the revelry, and the entertainment connected with modern carnivals, have got nothing to do with religion. In Gozo, the main Carnival is also held in Victoria, while at Nadur, a completely different carnival, a people's carnival is held. Floats, similar to the Carnival ones are used especially at the end of the football season when the victorious team returns to its hometown with the trophy, and is paraded around the streets on decorated floats. Such celebrations were already being carried out during the sixteenth century, when naval or military victories by the Christian powers in Europe were celebrated in Malta as well.

Carnival floats in Freedom Square, Valletta.

Colourful floats mixed with youthful enthusiasm

Large floats and fluorescent colours are the order of the day

A young lady dressed up for carnival

Harking back to old times … in noble costumes

Any eccentricity goes during carnival, at Nadur

Anything goes for carnival … let's take a ride on this old banger

MDINA AND RABAT

Human occupation of the area dates back to at least the second millennium BC. Mdina is Malta's old capital city, with Rabat being its suburb. A Bronze Age village is believed to have stood at one end of the hill where Mdina today lies. The area was subsequently occupied by the Phoenicians, the Carthaginians, and the Romans and became an important urban centre, with a dramatic increase in population. Melita, as the city was known during Roman times, was at least three times the size of present-day Mdina. There may have been a small fortified *oppidum*, while the rest of the city had its own fortifications.

Mdina remained the main centre of administration and the only fortified city in Malta till the sixteenth century. The fall of the Roman Empire had led to centuries of great uncertainties. The city was reduced in area to its present size probably during the Byzantine period. The character of the buildings was also changed, while the island's governing institutions and various important families established their buildings within the city. It remained the centre of administration throughout the medieval times, and also the site of the cathedral, the main church of the Maltese islands. All this changed in 1530 when the islands were ceded to the Order of St John which led to a diminution of the city's importance because the knights established themselves near the harbour area, first in Birgu and then in Valletta, their purposely-built city.

Under the Order, Mdina entered a period of decline and near abandonment by the central government as well as from the local population. The 1693 earthquake proved a blessing in disguise. The city suffered a lot of damage. Besides various private and public buildings and the fortifications that suffered damage, the cathedral suffered very extensive damages. This led to a renewal policy which was initiated by the Church which built a new baroque cathedral designed by Lorenzo Gafà. Grand Master Manoel de Vilhena rebuilt the main entrance and several public buildings. All of this restored the dignity of the city. Today, Mdina is one of the main attractions of the Maltese islands, with its old and medieval streets, the baroque cathedral and buildings, and the idyllic atmosphere that is felt while walking its streets.

Mdina, the old capital city of Malta

The monumental entrance to the courtyard of Vilhena Palace, Mdina

Rabat has also its own share of Mdina's history. With the reduction in the size of Mdina, Rabat started to gain its importance as the suburb of the main city. With the Religious Orders started arriving in medieval times, they set up their convents and churches within its limits. They are still there today functioning as centres of spirituality, art, and culture.

Places of interest include the fortifications that are a reminder of times past – and the times that these walls saw the enemy besieging them as in 1429 and 1551. The inhabitants always wanted to keep these fortifications in their best condition, as they were the only protection that could protect them from violent death or slavery. The entrance to the city of Mdina is a baroque creation, and dates to the building programme that took place at the beginning of the eighteenth century. One of the most interesting buildings in Mdina is the Vilhena Palace, built to the designs of François de Mondion on the orders of Grand Master Manoel de Vilhena. The palace was built in the French baroque style than prevalent in the islands. The yard in front of the building provides the guests with a theatre-like feeling. The eye is led towards the main entrance, with its columns, decorations, and the bronze bust of the grand master. On opposite sides the whole yard, there are two tiers of arcaded balconies, which accentuate the baroque theatricality.

The winding main street of Mdina follows the medieval street layout. A small church dedicated to St Agatha can be seen on turning the first corner. The present building replaced an earlier edifice towards the end of the seventeenth century. It was designed by Lorenzo Gafà, the Maltese architect who was very much involved in many important buildings in the second half of the seventeenth century. Adjacent to it, there is the nunnery and church of the Benedictine nuns who have been established in the city since the fourteenth century. The church holds several paintings by Mattia Preti and his bottega. Noble palaces vie with other less noble structures until one comes to the main square dominated by Lorenzo Gafà's masterpiece. Erected after the earthquake of 1693, the cathedral rises majestically above the whole city, and dwarfs all around it. However, the best view of the cathedral is enjoyed from outside Mdina itself, on the way up towards the city, where the dominating dome can be seen crowning the city. The cathedral deserves a visit, as it is one of the best-kept churches in the islands, besides the repository of very important works of art. The nearby Cathedral Museum is also worth a visit. This building was originally meant to be the seminary to train future priests. During the 1960s it was transformed into the Cathedral Museum, and is today considered as one of the most important artistic museums in Malta. There is a fine collection of paintings, silverware, church vestments, and a unique series of etchings by Albrecht Durer.

More medieval buildings can be seen in the street leading from the square to the belvedere, as well as in the other narrow streets. The doorways and the decorated windows are typical of the time. The local Globigerina limestone lends itself well to the creativity of the Maltese stonemasons, as they can easily work this soft yellowish stone. The so-called Norman House, the Palazzo Santa Sofia, and others are all worth a stop in front of them to admire their architectural details.

Right: The baroque cathedral at Mdina is surrounded by other interesting buildings dating from the 18th century down to the early 20th century.

The belvedere today is an unmissable stop for all visitors to Mdina, from where one can admire various towns and villages as well as the surrounding countryside. In times gone by this was the most important watch post of the area, as from there one can see a good part of the island's north-eastern coast. From there the signal was given when enemy ships were sighted.

Rabat is also interesting because of its many particular characteristics and historical buildings. There is the very important and highly interesting Domus Romana, which was a rich Roman town house, with particular mosaic pavements as well as several interesting Roman artefacts. Other important monuments dating to the Roman period are the many catacombs. The largest complex is St Paul's Catacombs, while the nearby St Agatha's Catacombs are very decorative. These catacombs were cemeteries used from the early fourth century AD onwards, because burial was not allowed within the city walls. The famous St Paul's Grotto, traditionally held to be the place where St Paul was kept during his three-month stay in 60 AD, is part of an important religious and architectural complex, which also includes the churches of St Paul and St Publius and the Wignacourt Museum.

On the outskirts of Rabat lies Buskett Gardens, a small wooded area which offers tranquillity and a place of shade throughout the year. The wooded area was a favourite hunting reserve for the grand masters. A small but well-fortified palace was erected in the 16th century, to be used as the grand masters' country retreat. It was also used as a retreat by the British governors, but today it is the official summer residence of the president of Malta. The Mnarja, one of Malta's most popular and traditional feasts which is held on 28 and 29 June, includes an agricultural show in the *Boschetto*, while on the eve of the 29th the wooded area is full with people singing, cooking, and eating fried rabbit. On the following day animal races are held at Rabat, and prizes are awarded for the best agricultural products entered in the competition.

Not far from Boschetto, there is also a complex of caves which, until the nineteenth century, was still inhabited by a large community who made a living by tending sheep and goats and looking after the fields. In the seventeenth century, the community reared animals to be sold to the people of Rabat and Mdina, but they themselves lived more on vegetables. Around the same cave complex, there are old Roman quarries, the enigmatic cart ruts (popularly known as Clapham Junction for their intricate layout), and even Punic tombs. This area is interesting from the archaeological, historical, and natural points of view.

The Rabat area is also popular for its many picturesque country walks. This is a highly agricultural area, with a variety of scenery that enhances the walks. The imposing Dingli Cliffs are popular with ramblers and offer many viewpoints that provide different scenarios, especially at sunset.

Left: The Mdina cathedral was rebuilt after the 1693 earthquake. In subsequent years it was lavishly decorated with monuments and other great works of art.

Right: The 18th-century baroque Seminary in Mdina, today houses the magnificent collection of the Cathedral Museum.

Top: The narrow and winding streets of Mdina offer a variety of window decorations, balconies, and doorways.

Left: The main entrance to the Corte Capitanale, today used as the office of the local council.

Top: In small narrow streets, one can still notice noble houses, with their typical medieval decorations.

Right: The recently restored Palazzo Falson. The ground floor is the older part of the building, while the upper storey was added in the late 19th century.

*Left: The baroque
entrance to
St Paul's Grotto,
where tradition
holds that the saint
passed his time
after his shipwreck.*

Right: The 17th-century St Paul's church, the parish of Rabat, erected over St Paul's Grotto.

Left: The Paleo-Christian St Paul's Catacombs, with an agape table in the foreground and the main hall of the complex.

Below: The sun lit cloister of the Dominican friars at Rabat.

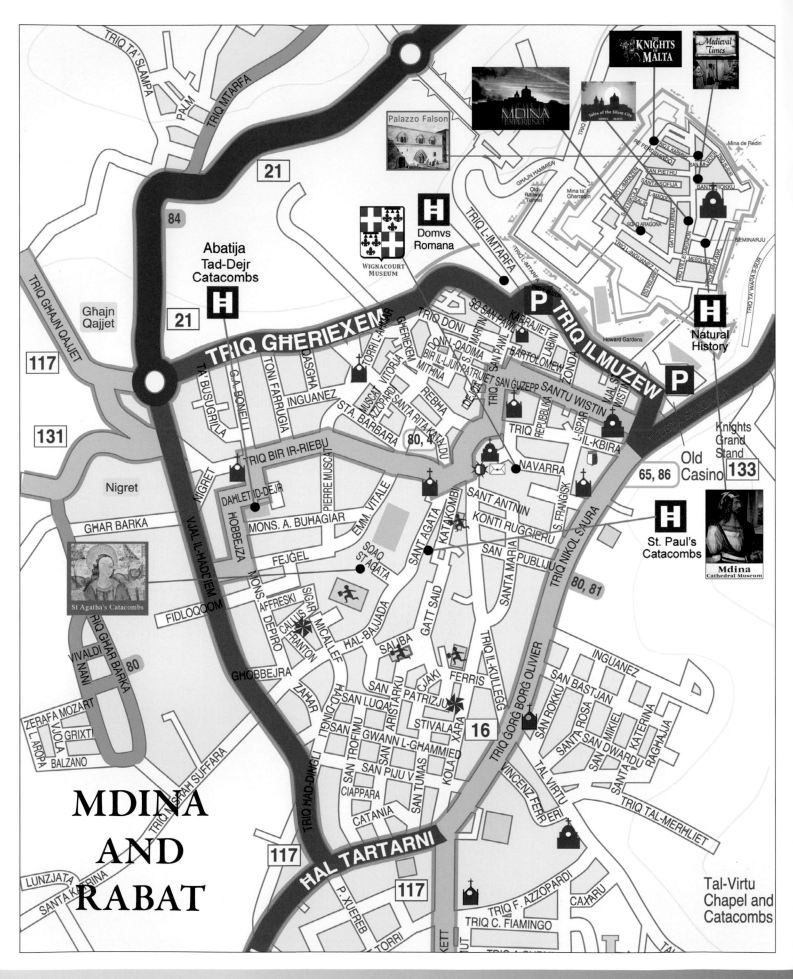

MDINA AND RABAT

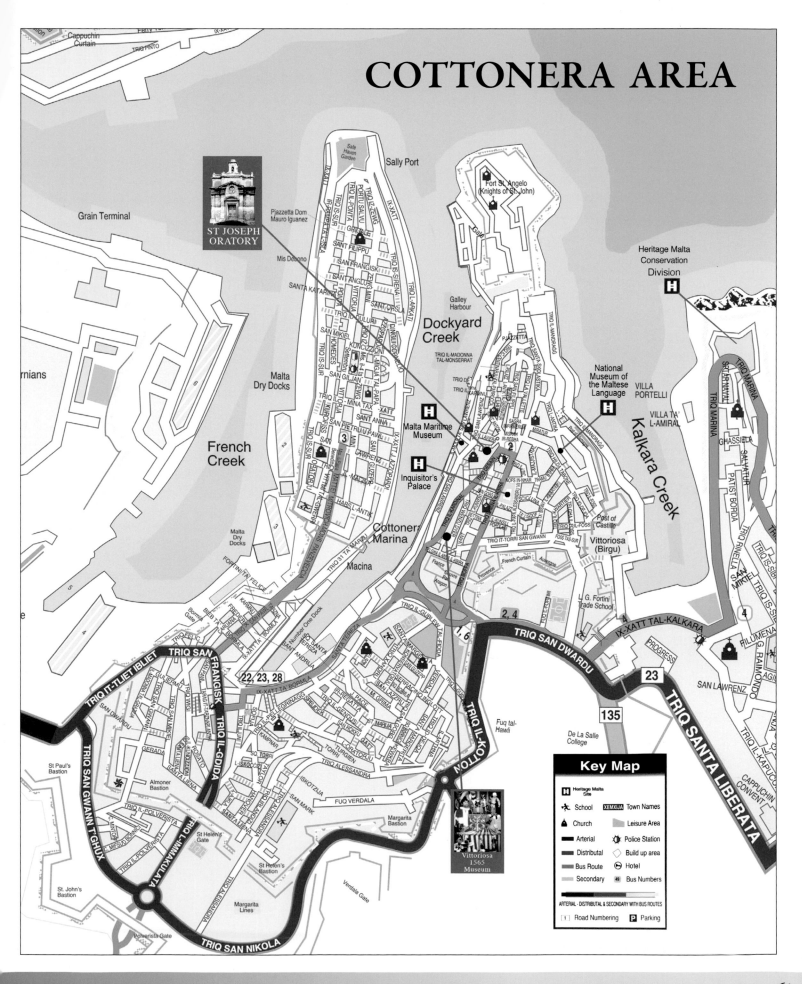

COTTONERA AREA

ST JOSEPH ORATORY

Grain Terminal

Cappuchin Curtain

TRIQ PINTO

Safe Haven Garden

Sally Port

Fort St. Angelo (Knights of St. John)

Gate

Pjazzetta Dom Mauro Iguanez

Mis Debono

Galley Harbour

Dockyard Creek

Heritage Malta Conservation Division

Malta Dry Docks

National Museum of the Maltese Language

VILLA PORTELLI

VILLA TA' L-AMIRAL

Kalkara Creek

French Creek

Malta Maritime Museum

Inquisitor's Palace

Post of Castille

Vittoriosa (Birgu)

Malta Dry Docks

Cottonera Marina

Macina

French Curtain

L. G. Fortini Trade School

2, 4

IX-XATT TAL-KALKARA

TRIQ SAN DWARDU

TRIQ IT-TLIET IBLIET

TRIQ SAN FRANGISK

22, 23, 28

1, 6

23

135

TRIQ IL-KOTTON

Fuq tal-Hawli

De La Salle College

TRIQ SANTA LIBERATA

St Paul's Bastion

Almoner Bastion

St Helen's Gate

Margarita Bastion

Vittoriosa 1565 Museum

CAPPUCHIN CONVENT

TRIQ SAN GWANN T'GHUX

St Helen's Bastion

Verdala Gate

St. John's Bastion

Margarita Lines

Polverista Gate

TRIQ SAN NIKOLA

Key Map

H Heritage Malta Site			
School		**XEMXIJA** Town Names	
Church		Leisure Area	
Arterial		Police Station	
Distribual		Build up area	
Bus Route		Hotel	
Secondary		**49** Bus Numbers	

ARTERIAL - DISTRIBUAL & SECONDARY WITH BUS ROUTES

1	Road Numbering	**P** Parking

61

COTTONERA AREA

It is traditionally held that the Phoenicians or the Romans had a temple, or temples, built where Fort St Angelo stands. The Arabs are traditionally held to have built the first fortification in the area. These fortifications continued to be enlarged and bettered over the centuries, until the Second World War, when they were still the centre of the defence of the harbour area.

The area is locally referred to as the Cottonera, for the simple reason that in 1670, owing to the fear of an Ottoman invasion, a long line of fortifications were built on the landward side to encircle the three cities. This was meant to provide defence to the population of the cities and to the country people living in the nearby villages. These fortifications were initiated by Grand Master Nicholas Cotoner, hence the name Cottonera Lines. Besides these fortifications, there are individual lines of bastions and curtains that offer protection to the individual cities as well. Passing through these defences, one can appreciate better what it was like to live in those days when one lived in daily fear of one's life.

The city of Senglea (*Isla* in Maltese) offers a magnificent view of the Grand Harbour and Valletta from the garden situated at the end of the peninsula. One should admire the look-out post, considered the best existing example in Maltese fortifications. The present parish church is a modern reconstruction as the original one was destroyed in the Second World War. One can understand why Senglea was so heavily bombed, as beneath its fortifications there is still the Malta Drydocks. A walk along the shore will provide different vistas of the other cities and of the creek that separates all Three Cities and which today is the site of a yacht marina where many mega-yachts winter every year.

The main point of interest of Cospicua (Bormla in Maltese) is the parish church dedicated to the Immaculate Conception. The best time to view the beauty of this church is either during the feast day on 8 December or during Holy Week. The church is richly decorated with various religious vestments as well as artistic statuary and paintings. Near the official entrance of Cospicua there is the seventeenth-century baroque gateway to the Sta Margerita Lines.

continues on page 66

The Three Cities, with Valletta in the background

A pupier-mâché statue of GM Cotoner in front of St Helen's Gate

Top: Fort St Angelo and the
Grand Harbour entrance.

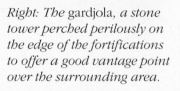

Right: The gardjola, a stone
tower perched perilously on
the edge of the fortifications
to offer a good vantage point
over the surrounding area.

Left: A Maltese
luzzu with
the Senglea
fortifications in
the background.

Right: Vittoriosa is renowned for its large and exquisite banners used as street decorations.

Left: Cospicua parish church dominating the skyline, and the nearby marina.

Bottom: The 16th-century ribbed vault architecture at the Inquisitor's Palace, Vittoriosa.

The Birgu fortifications

Rock cut shelters used during Second World War

The richly-decorated interior of St Lawrence parish church

continues from page 62

Birgu, or Vittoriosa as it is officially known, may have already been inhabited in prehistoric times. It is also believed that at the extreme end of the promontory, which juts into the middle of the Grand Harbour, there could have been a temple first erected by the Phoenicians. The main fortifications of the city are impressive. The entrance is a throw-back to the old medieval system, when entrances were made up of more than one actual gateway. Here one needs to pass through three different gateways, each one well defended and protected by the bastions behind it. Managing to win through these entrances was indeed a very difficult enterprise. Note that the fortifications were carved out of the living rock, with only a few courses of dressed stone placed on the upper part in order to provide a better alignment. The ditches of the city were also used during the Second World War by those who did not wish to leave their hometown. Rock-cut shelters were dug into the bastions and a labyrinth of these shelters has recently been restored and is open to the public. Inside one can feel what the Maltese experienced when they lived in the most dangerous area of the island and somehow managed to get through years of aerial bombardment.

The main church of Vittoriosa is dedicated to St Lawrence, the patron saint of the city, on whose feast day the whole city is richly decorated and *en fete*. The church was already standing before the arrival of the knights in 1530, when it was then taken over by the Order and turned into its conventual church. Various interior decorations were added to by the Grand Masters and the Order, and all the important functions associated with a religious and a military order, were held inside it. When the Order officially moved to Valletta in 1571, this church became once more the parish church of Vittoriosa. With the subsequent arrival of the inquisitor to Malta and the setting up of his office in one of the palaces of Vittoriosa, the church was used by this important church dignitary till the end of the eighteenth century. In the seventeenth century the church was rebuilt to the designs of Vittoriosa-born Lorenzo Gafà, one of the best local architects. The church has various artistic treasures, the most important being the titular painting by Mattia Preti and the titular statue which is carried shoulder-high during the annual procession. A small church museum can be visited inside St Joseph's Oratory, next to the main church. This museum contains various relics of the knights and other recent items of interest connected with the church and Vittoriosa. There one can also see the actual sword used by de Valette during the Great Siege of 1565 and his magisterial hat.

Vittoriosa was the seat of the Order's government for 41 years but afterwards it retained some importance as the navy still kept its arsenals and offices there. Walk around the city streets one can appreciate its varied architectural treasures. The other large church in Vittoriosa is a modern structure rebuilt after the Second World War when the former building was destroyed. This church is administered by the Dominican Order who was established in the city early in the sixteenth century. Opposite the church lies the Inquisitor's Palace, a labyrinth of passages, rooms, prison cells, and a highly-interesting display of various items of ethnographic interest. The palace is going through various restorations, but it is still open to the public. Within the older part of the city, there is the first hospital the Order built, used today by cloistered nuns. The church attached to the nunnery was built by Lorenzo Gafà and the titular painting is by Mattia Preti. The knights built their auberges in the narrow and winding streets soon after their arrival in Malta. Although these small town houses passed through considerable changes, two of them are almost as they were originally. The best example is the English auberge which is used as an area library and as a front office by the local council. The Armoury was used as a depository for the arms and armour during the year, as no one could carry arms, if not in case of an emergency. The knights had several such small area armouries from where arms and armour were kept to be distributed to the local people. The winding streets offer a variety of buildings, from a medieval window to modern structures and decorations. A number of wine bars have also been established in old houses, still retaining their architectural details. The fortifications that surround a good part of the city offer many good views of the surrounding area. Along Galley Creek is now a modern yacht marina, which continues the tradition of offering shelter to those that seek its calm waters.

Kalkara is the small fishing village that originally lay in the shadows of the fortifications of the Three Cities. It has become a popular residential zone of this area. Most of the buildings are modern, and even the church was erected in the 1950s. At the tip of the peninsula, where there used to be a seventeenth-century country residence of an Italian knight, Fra Bichi, the British naval authorities decided to erect a naval hospital, which functioned till the 1970s. Today, it houses Heritage Malta's Centre for Restoration. There is also a small sandy bay under the shadow of Fort Ricasoli which was built in 1670. Within the fort were built the film sets for Gladiator and Troy, two Hollywood blockbusters that were filmed at the Mediterranean Film Studios.

The tribunal at the Inquisitor's Palace

The Auberge of England in the Medieval part of Birgu

Bighi Naval Hospital, today used as a Centre for Restoration

Right: The Cottonera Lines, the Malta Shipyards, and the Grand Harbour.

Top: A detail of the 18th-century ship-of-the-line model at the Maritime Museum.

Right: Freedom Monument, commemorating the departure of the British Forces.

Wrought-iron works.

A steady hand for the decoration of small models

Pottery is hand-painted to give it that individual look

Filigree work

The art of glass blowing has been retained

Colourful finished glass products

The Crafts Village

The Ta' Qali Crafts Village is located in the old disused airfield, lying just beneath the watchful eyes of the cathedral and bastions of Mdina, and very close to the impressive dome of the Mosta Rotunda. It is immediately clear that this village was set up in an old airfield, when one starts to look at the various huts, which are typically associated with airfields. The largest hut has been turned into the very successful Mdina Glass factory. Here one can not only buy the material that has been produced, but can also follow the whole process of the production of a glass item.

On the other side of this large hangar, there is the cluster of small huts, all catering for different and specialized craft material. In most cases the actual craftsmen tend to be working in the backrooms of these shops, so the visitor can see the work being done and created in front of him. Amongst the most interesting and typical souvenirs of the islands, there is lace, a favourite with Maltese ladies as well as for giving out as gifts; pottery, present in Malta since the arrival of the first Man on the islands around 7,000 years ago; and filigree work. The latter could have been introduced into Malta by the Phoenicians who were renowned for their intricate designs of their jewellery. Although only a few pieces were discovered in Malta dating from this period, the present-day examples have been popular with all females since the time of the knights of St John. In various paintings of the period females are depicted wearing such earrings and jewellery.

There are a number of other small shops selling all kinds of souvenirs. Besides the one at Ta` Qali, there is another small crafts village in Gozo.

Giving the final touches to a pottery jar before firing

The earliest clay female figurine from the Skorba huts (background aerial photo), Mgarr

ARCHAEOLOGY

Since Man started to build boats and venture out from the coast, it was possible to reach the Maltese islands from nearby Sicily. One can imagine the first human crossing over the channel, when he saw new land for the first time. Not knowing its size and whether it was inhabited, curiosity led them to finally make the crossing. What they discovered seems to have been to their liking, as they settled on the Maltese islands around 5000 BC, bringing over with them their various innovative methods of living. Community life was introduced, as well as farming.

The earliest traces of these first humans on the islands have been identified inside Għar Dalam and other caves, as well as at Skorba village. Living in caves has never been contrary to the mentality of various Mediterranean communities as can be seen till this very day in various parts of the region. With limestone being common around the Mediterranean Sea, there are also numerous natural water-worn caves. The soft stone also led to the people to start manipulating this very important natural resource leading to the erection of small huts, walls, and even a village at Skorba. These people also introduced farming, bringing over with them different seeds and domesticated animals.

Għar Dalam is one of the most intriguing sites to visit with regards to the early prehistory of the islands. The first humans who established themselves in Malta settled in this cave. Beneath the same occupational level of these people, there were discovered a number of stratigraphies that indicated the formation of the islands. In these layers the fossilized remains of a number of prehistoric animals, namely foxes, wolves, brown bears, hippopotami, and elephants have been identified. Different species of the last two animals were discovered in the lower layers, the most interesting being the dwarf-sized elephants, which have been given the scientific name of *elephas melitensis*.

In due time these early farmers became more confident in the use of the local Globigerina Limestone and started to experiment in the construction of bigger sanctuaries. From small trefoil temples, they ended up building the impressive temples that we still admire. A good number of well preserved temple sites have been identified. The main sites of the period are the underground Ħal Saflieni, and the temples of Ħaġar Qim, Mnajdra, Tarxien, and Ġgantija in Gozo. These temples are considered as the oldest free-standing buildings in the world, and it is no wonder that UNESCO has thought it fit to consider these remains as World Heritage Sites.

Decorated handles found at Għar Dalam (background photo)

The 'Holy of Holies', Ħal Saflieni Hypogeum

A pair of the inner apses of the Tarxien central temple

Stone altars at the entrance of an apse at Ħaġar Qim temples

Ħal Saflieni is unique. It is the only underground complex that has survived from this period. Excavated into the live rock, starting around 3500 BC, this complex began when the prehistoric community seem to have decided to continue to tunnel deeper into the earth to extend their cemeteries, which is what the Hypogeum effectively is. The underground complex gives us also a very good idea of how the above ground temples would have looked like in their heyday. The wall decorations with red ochre and the architectural features are all repeated in the temples. Various items were discovered there, the most important being the small terracotta statuette of the Sleeping Lady, a masterpiece of prehistoric art, which can be admired in the Museum of Archaeology in Valletta.

The **Tarxien** complex boasts of at least four temples. It is an excellent place to admire the various temples and understand better how the different architectural styles developed. The earliest temple dates to around 3200 BC and it is made up mostly of small stones. The second temple is a completely different with large stones being used in its construction. Its builders were more confident with the techniques of stone-building and they had mastered it completely. The third temple is more elaborate. The façade is impressive, even though most of what can be seen is a reconstruction. The central court seems to have been used for mass celebrations, as the temples apparently all sported such open courts in front of their main entrance. The interior, and especially the first two semi-circular rooms, or apses as they are called, are considered as the most decorated of all temples. The various stones have got spiral designs in relief, as well as animals, and there is also a copy of a colossal statue of a human figure. Although usually referred to as the Fat Lady, there is nothing to indicate its sex. The last temple is another jewel of prehistoric temple building, with its perfectly lined uprights, pavements, and other decorations.

The two sets of temple complexes that are to be found on the south-western part of the island, **Ħaġar Qim** and **Mnajdra**, are also highly interesting. Ħaġar Qim can be reached easily, while Mnajdra lies at the bottom of a hill, but there one can enjoy a scenario that cannot be found near any other prehistoric temple. Ħaġar Qim does not follow the usual temple plans as, when it was being enlarged over the centuries; further additions disrupted the typical plan. Yet, all the features can be seen here as well, with the façade, the large megaliths, the apses, and the interior decorations. Around the outside retaining wall there are other remains which are still unexplained. The walk towards the Mnajdra Temples presents one with a scenario nearer to that of the prehistoric communities. The second of the three temples here contains what is considered as the earliest calendar in stone in the world. It seems to have been built in order to indicate the start of the four seasons, as the rays of the rising sun hit certain corners in the temple to indicate that a new season was starting. These phenomena can still be observed.

Gozo has the impressive **Ġgantija** temples. These consist of two temples abutting one other. The larger is the earlier, and the inner three apses make up the first temple built on the site. Later on, two other apses were added, while another new temple was erected next to the older structure. The style of building in this temple is completely different. Besides a few dressed corner stones, the others are completely left in their raw state and are more akin to the Cyclopean style that was to be dominant in the following period, the Bronze Age, rather than to the Temple Period. Yet, the remains of its façade are most impressive and rise to quite a height. The scaffolding that can be seen is part of the research that is going on to find the proper means to preserve these structures for future generations.

Other prehistoric temples that have survived in Malta are the **Skorba** temples and the **Ta' Ħaġrat** temples lying not far away at Mġarr. Nearer the Grand Harbour there are the Kordin III temples, while several other remains can be seen in the countryside.

Besides these main prehistoric remains, the islands also boast of a number of minor sites. There are the small upright stones which are referred to as menhirs. The local examples cannot be compared with their European counterparts, as these examples lack decoration, and no pottery has ever been discovered associated with them to help date them properly. A number of these upright stones are to be found in various locations around the islands. Another type of minor prehistoric remains are the so-called dolmens, structures which are similar to European examples, but much smaller in size. They seem to have been used as burial places, although once more not enough pottery evidence has been discovered to really date them. The examples in Malta are mostly made up of a large block of stone, placed above a number of small stones. It is thought that pottery urns full of cremated remains were buried beneath the large stone.

The most enigmatic archaeological remains in the islands are the so-called cart-ruts. These are ruts carved into the solid rock, always in pairs. They seem to be similar in concept to the modern railway tracks. Some examples stretch for quite a distance, but it is still difficult to know where they are leading to. At the same time it is also a mystery what kind of loads they carried. If one knew what load, then maybe it would be easier to identify their period, as well as the type of

continues on page 78

The impressive walls of one of the side apses at Mnajdra south temple

The façade of Ta' Ħaġrat temple, Mġarr

The dolmans at Mosta, remains from the Bronze Age

Left: The impressive cyclopean type of architecture of the façade of Ġgantija Temples.

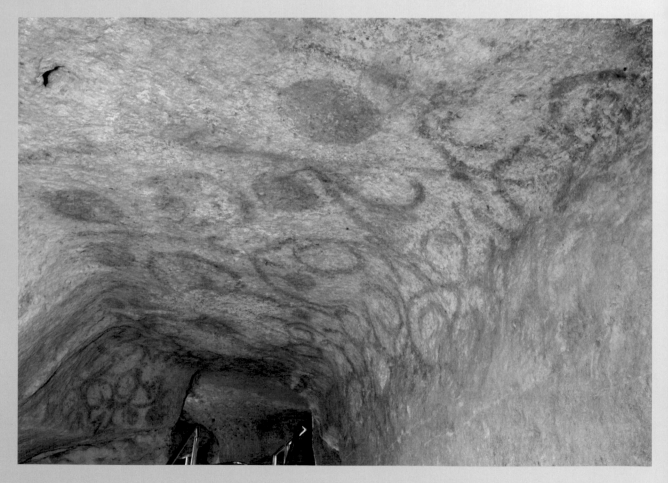

Right: Red ochre decorates the ceiling of one of the chambers inside the Hal Saflieni Hypogeum.

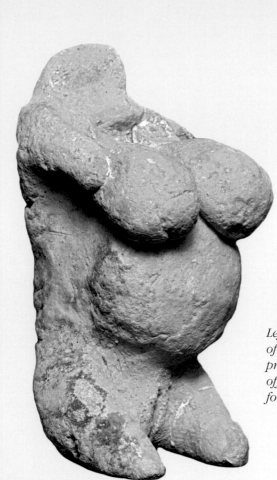

Left: A representation of a pregnant female, probably a votive offering to the deities, found at Mnajdra.

Top: One of the most exquisite small figurines of Prehistoric Malta, the Sleeping Lady from Hal Saflieni.

Top: Stone seated corpulent figures found at Ħaġar Qim.

Right: The Venus of Malta, a figure of a nude, discovered at Ħaġar Qim.

The enigmatic cart-ruts at San Pawl Tat-Tarġa

The shaft of a Punic rock-cut tomb

Part of a mosaic pavement from the Domus Romana

continues from page 75

vehicle used. The ruts are V-shaped and they are mostly very similar in depth and in width. The cart-ruts can be seen in various localities, the most interesting are those at San Pawl Tat-Tarġa, limits of Naxxar; those near the Buskett Gardens, known as the Clapham Junction; and those at Dwejra at Gozo. If all of the above is not enough, there are still debates with regards to which period they should be associated with. Some believe that they are prehistoric, while others date them to antiquity, either during the Phoenicians, Punic, or Roman times. Several quarries which are datable to the Roman period have been identified close by the cart-ruts at Buskett.

From antiquity there are a number of important sites of great archaeological interest. Amongst the most common are the various small and individual rock-cut tombs, the earliest datable to the Phoenicians. Close by to the above-mentioned cart ruts at Buskett, are several rock-cut tombs which could take two corpses at a time. These tombs are usually studied in order to indicate where the first Phoenician communities settled and their way of life.

The Phoenicians introduced writing and coinage to the islands. They occupied the centrally-located town of Mdina and built a ring of walls to protect it from marauding pirates. They also must have occupied coastal areas for their maritime activity. The Carthaginians retained the same mentality, although they introduced countryside residences. These country farmhouses had residential quarters as well as working areas. The islands were attacked by the emerging Roman power, and finally conquered in 218 BC, during the Second Punic War. This led to a new type of government and mentality, although the culture remained very much tied to that of North African, as had been the case in the previous centuries.

The remains dating to the Roman period are few but impressive. The most important is the Domus Romana, a town house built within the fortified town of Melita, the name of the island and of the main town during Roman times. This house's most impressive mosaic pavement indicates the wealth and status of its owners. The best part of it has survived the passage of time practically intact, even though, during the tenth and eleventh centuries, a Muslim cemetery was sited above the ruins of the house.

The pavements indicate that these were made by a very able itinerant artist who was influenced by the Hellenistic style. The various rooms were richly decorated, although some of them are very much in ruins. The centrally-placed peristyle was surrounded by 16 stone columns, of which only fragments survive. The museum, which has been set up around this palatial building, narrates the discovery of the site and the Muslim cemetery. One can see Muslim tomb-stones, domestic materials associated with the Romans, large statues, and fragments of mosaics. Behind the museum, one can get a glimpse of part of the Roman city of Melita.

There are at least two other important Roman sites. One is the Roman Baths, which at the moment are being restored. The baths consist of a complex of various rooms, typical of the Roman baths system. These were erected in the vicin-ity of a natural source, and the water was then channelled towards the complex. The complex includes changing rooms, the various rooms associated with the Roman ritual of taking baths, latrines, and a piscine. The floors of most rooms are still in a fairly good condition and are covered by mosaics.

At Burmarrad, limits of St Paul's Bay, there are the re-mains of a countryside villa. This area was in use as early as the Bronze Age and it was also occupied during subsequent periods. The Roman erected a countryside villa or farm-house, with an attached working area. Local tradition holds the villa to have belonged to Publius, the Maltese governor in 60 AD when St Paul was shipwrecked on the islands. It is held that Publius welcomed Paul and his companions here and it was also here that Paul healed Publius's ailing father, which led to the governor converting to Christianity. During medieval times a small church was erected over the opening of the well, found at this villa, which was reputedly used by Paul to baptize Publius. The church was rebuilt more than once. The complex is managed by Heritage Malta and is only open on request.

Other important archaeological remains dating to this period are the various catacombs. The most impressive are those in the Rabat area, especially the two large complexes known as St Paul's and St Agatha's catacombs respectively. These underground cemeteries are associated with the early Christian communities, but they were used by all the differ-ent religious communities on the islands. The underground complexes are interesting, as they clearly show that even then there were tombs meant for the rich and others for poor families. The decorations, the size, and the elaborate structure of some of the tombs are quite varied and one should not miss visiting at least one of these complexes.

While for the Roman period, the best museum collec-tion is the Domus Romana at Rabat, for the prehistoric remains it is best to visit the National Museum of Archaeol-ogy, Valletta, where one can admire the original prehistoric masterpieces. Gozo's archaeological museum boasts another good collection, albeit a small one, of prehistoric, classical, and medieval artefacts.

The ruins of San Pawl Milqi

The decorated side walls of the Salina catacombs

Frescoes on the walls of St Agatha's cave church, Rabat

Left: Disk idols from the Bronze Age, the last period of the Maltese prehistoric sequence.

Left: A reconstructed marble statue of Emperor Claudius, exhibited at the Domus Romana.

Left: The Phoenician symbol of Osiris, who protected people against bad luck, and which is still to be seen on Maltese fishing boats.

Below: Multi-coloured faience glass phials dating from the Punic period of Malta.

Top and right: The lead seal from the 9th-century of Theophylact the Archon, found in Gozo in 1960.

Top: The Maimuna tombstone, traditionally held to have been discovered in Gozo, today exhibited at the Gozo Museum of Archaeology, on the Citadel.

Below: A small box of relics, the Hagiothecium *dating from c.1340, brought over from Rhodes by the knights of St John. Now at the Cathedral Museum, Mdina.*

Top: The marble coat-of-arms of the Inguanes noble family, affixed on the inside of the main gate of Mdina, the old capital city and the stronghold of the family.

Mosta

Mosta is thought to derive its name from its central location on the island. This was one of the villages which became popular after the knights of St John built permanent coastal defences, as it had always been prone to attacks by pirates up to that time. A couple of legends remind us of those times. One of the most famous is the Bride of Mosta which states that while a bride was preparing to go to meet with her future husband a group of pirates who had landed in the vicinity raided the house where the females were gathered together and carried them away. The groom vowed to get his bride back. It took him many years to find her and she died soon afterwards in his hands, knowing that he had never abandoned her. A garden situated on the escarpment looking down towards the valley of Burmarrad, and taking in the fortifications of the nineteenth-century Victoria Lines, is named after the Bride of Mosta. Another lovely legend is connected with the small church dedicated to Our Lady of Hope.

Mosta was elevated to a parish in the early seventeenth century. This led to a bigger church to be built, which was eventually engulfed by the new huge Rotunda in the nineteenth century. The new church was quite an achievement. The building, which took over 30 years to build, was carried out without any scaffolding around the older church so that the parishioners would not miss out on going to their religious services. The architect was the Maltese-born Giorgio Grognet de Vassè who suggested the idea to build a church like the Pantheon, the only one of its kind in Malta at that time. Owing to the vicinity of Ta' Qali airfield, during the Second World War Mosta lay in the path of airplanes attacking the airfield. During one such raid in 1942, several bombs were dropped around the Rotunda, with one actually piercing the dome. Although there were about 300 people inside the church, the bomb failed to explode and no one was injured. The dome suffered only slight damage and remained intact, something which the people considered a miracle. The interior of the church is impressive. Inside the sacristy there is a replica of the bomb that had pierced the dome.

The streets of Mosta offer various attractive architectural features. Mosta has also got its own particular prehistoric remains and areas of natural beauty. The dolmens consist of a flat slab of stone resting on two blocks of stones which were probably used for burial purposes. There is also the impressive Fort Mosta which forms part of the Victoria Lines fortifications, built by the British to offer protection to their ever-important naval establishment in and around the Grand Harbour of Valletta.

Fort Mosta, part of the Victoria Lines of Fortifications, a 19th-century defensive work

The impressive interior of the Mosta Rotunda, built in the 19th-century

A character during the Good Friday procession at Żejtun

Devotees during the Good Friday procession at Żebbuġ

One of the statues during the devotional procession at Paola

The Holy Week Pageant at Mosta

Running with the statue of the Risen Christ at Bormla

A lavishly laid-out Last Supper display at Valletta

84

Holy Week

The dominant religion of the Maltese islands is Catholicism. It is obvious that there would be a number of religious feasts held during the year. Some of these religious celebrations are held during Holy Week, which is a popular activity that commemorates the passion and resurrection of Christ. During the days leading up to Holy Week, various organizations, clubs, and individuals start preparing for the processions and other activities. Small exhibitions are held in hallways, garages, and even in the small churches in the villages. Other exhibitions depict the Last Supper, while all kinds of innovative and creative exhibitions are now being regularly organized.

Some parish churches organize the solemn procession with a number of statues depicting different episodes from the Passion of Christ. These processions are popular baroque manifestations which are very typical of the islands. The numbers of participants, helpers behind the scenes, and visitors that flock to watch the whole proceedings are an indication that these are still very popular with locals and tourists alike. The apex of these celebrations is reached on Sunday morning when the Church celebrates the resurrection of Christ. At the end of the mass, in certain villages, processions are held with the statue of the Risen Christ. In some places, these statues are not only just carried around the streets, but usually the bearers run with the statue for some distance to indicate the victory of Christ over Death. During these processions children hold high their *figolla [**Top; next to title**]*, a sweet pastry delicacy typical of the time, to be blessed by the statue of the Risen Christ.

The baroque manifestation of the Holy Week procession compliments the baroque façade of the Naxxar parish church

Marsaxlokk & Marsascala

The bay of Marsaxlokk, one of the largest in Malta, has several villages around its shores. The most picturesque is the one that carries the same name of the bay, Marsaxlokk. Visiting the largest fishing village of Malta is always an experience, at all times of day. During the week there is a small flea market, selling various Maltese products. One can enjoy an easy stroll along the wharf and enjoy the scenery as well as the fishermen at work, mending their nets or preparing for a fishing trip. On Sunday the whole village becomes a market. The stalls are augmented by a large number of fish stalls where one can actually buy fresh fish and other sea creatures. The atmosphere is quite impressive. The large number of tourists and locals that visit this place on Sunday makes this village very lively and a place not to be missed.

Almost all the various colourful fishing boats of various sizes sport the talismanic eye of Osiris for good luck. This tradition may date back to the Phoenicians, who must have had an important settlement close by. Indeed the archaeological site of Tas-Silġ is a most important one which, however, it is not open to the public owing to ongoing excavations. The devout people of Marsaxlokk have also set up a stone statue of St Andrew, the patron saint of fishermen. This statue can be seen overseeing the harbour activity, as does the stone statue of Our Lady riding on a *luzzu* (the Maltese fishing boat) which can be seen on the frontispiece of the parish church. Fort St Lucian, standing on the high middle promontory of the bay, built to offer protection to the villagers, is today part of the Ministry of Fisheries and carries out research on fish-farming, an important industry for Malta.

Marsascala is another small fishing village that has been developed as a tourist resort. Evening strolls along the wharf are very popular. The village is popular during winter time as it is less chaotic. The countryside around it offers good walks, with excellent seascapes. The unique Mamo Tower, a seventeenth-century family fortified building overlooking the adjacent St Thomas Bay, is worth a visit.

Preparing the boats and the tackle for a day out at sea, Marsaxlokk

Left: The idyllic setting of a quiet day at Marsaskala Bay.

Below left and bottom: Cleaning fish for the clients on Sunday morning at the fish market, Marsaxlokk. The choice of the best freshly-caught fish on Sunday morning at the Marsaxlokk fish market.

Below: St Thomas tower, one of the 17th-century fortifications, Marsaskala.

Wied iż-Żurrieq

On the south-western coast, one meets with a different coastal scenario. The cliffs are higher, and the sea seems to be deeper and a deeper blue. The cliffs contain a number of naturally-worn caves which were created by the rushing waves over the millennia. One of the characteristic villages of this area is Żurrieq which boasts of old buildings dating back to antiquity and several churches which are veritable architectural treasures. The small churches have all got their charm, while the recently-restored ones are little gems. The parish church is an important ecclesiastical building that deserves a visit. It has impressive artistic treasures, in particular a number of good canvases by the Italian baroque master Mattia Preti.

Another interesting architectural treasure is the eighteenth-century windmill which has recently been restored and is open to the public on arrangement with the local council. During its restoration there was discovered a complex of catacombs – an early Christian cemetery.

Not far from the village there is the typically Mediterranean inlet of Wied iż-Żurrieq, which is rightly famous for the short boat ride to the famous Blue Grotto and other small caves near it. On the way one should appreciate the imposing natural scenery, as well as the play of light of the coral in the caves. Out in the open sea, there is the small islet of Filfla which used to have a small cave church on it, built by fishermen as a votive thanksgiving. In the 1950s the islet was used for target practice by the British navy but it is today a nature reserve. A little farther along the coast, there is Għar Lapsi, another similar inlet which is a popular bathing place for many Maltese families. The large cave near the sea, a very Mediterranean characteristic, offers welcome shelter from the summer sun while the sea is exceptionally inviting and clear.

At both Wied iż-Żurrieq and Għar Lapsi, the fish restaurants are very inviting.

Wied iż-Żurrieq where boats and swimmers enjoy the deep blue sea

*Left: Tourism is one of
the mainstays of the
Maltese economy; shops
at Wied iż-Żurrieq.*

*Top: Diving at such
clear blue seas is ideal
for the enthusiasts.*

Below: Il-Ħnejja – *The
arched entrance to the
famous Blue Grotto.*

Sliema & St Julians

These villages are the trend-setting area of the islands. Almost uninhabited till the mid-nineteenth century, the area then started to attract people deciding to move away from the busy life of Valletta and the inner harbour area. The British authorities found this area rich in unoccupied land, and started building barracks and other ancillary buildings for their troops and subsequently for the families. The more British soldiers started to be billeted here, the more Maltese started to be attracted to the area, and this led to its fast development.

The area has several interesting fortifications. The impressive Fort Tignè is being engulfed by modern development which should, however, respect the architectural features of an eighteenth-century defensive work. Another small nineteenth-century fortification, Sliema Point Battery, with its eye-catching neo-gothic architecture, is a catering establishment. The small solitary seventeenth-century tower has been a feature of Tower Road ever since it was erected. Other fortifications have been integrated into the ever-expanding construction work in the area.

Top: Il-Fortizza, a 19th-century British coastal fortification, converted into a restaurant.

Other interesting architectural features are partly connected with nineteenth-century tastes. There are churches and impressive buildings. Besides the military barracks, which have given an identity of its own to the area, there are the palatial buildings like the Balluta Mansions *[detail above]* as well as the Villa Rosa. At the turn of the twentieth century, affluent Maltese families started building summer houses along the shoreline of Sliema and St Julian's. These tended to be two-storey houses built facing the open sea, so that their owners could spend the summer evenings walking along the front. This idyllic lifestyle changed with the Second World War. Families moved permanently to their summer houses, as they were deemed to be quite safe from aerial bombing, while many other families were billeted to this zone. The population increased dramatically and it did not decrease with the end of the war. With the growth in tourism from the late 1950s onwards, both towns experienced considerable development that is still going on.

The first hotels of the 1960s were built here. What used to be country residences became high-rise buildings, modern shops, and other amenities that go hand in hand with the tourist product. One can appreciate all of this when one manages to take a walk, either in the morning or in the evening, along the two towns. During the morning the shops representing all the big international brands offer their wares for sale, while in the evening there is all kind of entertainment going on. The most popular area is Paceville.

Here it is possible to visit small bars where the old village mentality still lingers on, and also more complex and elegant high-style dining establishments. There are all kinds of pubs, bars, restaurants, and take-aways that offer all kind of food and entertainment. This is the area where the Maltese mingle freely with the tourists and where one can notice the latest impressive architectural creations. There is a small marina nestling in the shadow of the first real high-rise building in Malta, modern churches with corners for private prayers, hotels, and the latest in modern entertainment venues.

From Sliema one can take a boat ride either around the Grand Harbour, cross over to Valletta by ferry, or have a relaxing trip around Malta with stops for lunch at Comino's Blue Lagoon where one can also enjoy a swim in the clearest blue sea you could ever imagine. The shoreline is also attractive to swimmers.

Top: The sun setting on Balluta Bay.

Right: One of the 13 coastal towers built by GM de Redin.

Top: Strolling along the inner part of Spinola Bay.

Left: Modern buildings front the sea at Sliema next to Independence Gardens.

Top: Paceville – a Mecca for shopping and nightlife.

Right: Portomaso – modern amenities in beautiful surroundings.

Architecture

The Maltese islands are an architectural paradise. The various powers that occupied the islands throughout the last 7,000 years have all left their mark, one way or another. The most impressive architectural remains must surely be the prehistoric temples, which have been called 'the oldest free-standing buildings in the world'. One can appreciate the techniques used by these prehistoric builders, even though they lacked the proper tools to erect such impressive structures. Chronologically, the next architectural gems are from the Roman period, with the most important being the Domus at Rabat and the Roman Baths, limits of Mġarr.

Medieval architecture can be mostly seen at Mdina or in the various older village cores that still abound. The small houses have been lost, but the impressive palaces built by the well-to-do and the noble families have survive. Some of these were also added to during the subsequent centuries but at least their architecture was retained. The two-mullioned windows and the pointed arches are typical of this period. Something similar can be seen at Birgu, especially inside the Inquisitor's Palace. Some churches dating from this period have survived as well, although they are not amongst the most impressive.

The Baroque period must surely be referred to as the Golden Age of Malta. The building of Valletta in the sixteenth century led to the military and religious Order of St John to set up its headquarters there. After settling down, the knights started to add to their buildings, or even pull them down and rebuild them. Foreign architects who were invited over to Malta, together with local talent, erected buildings like the auberge of Castile in Valletta (Andrea Belli), the cathedral in Mdina (Lorenzo Gafà), and various other palaces all over the islands. While all of this public building was being carried out, whole systems of fortifications were being planned and built all over the islands. The urban conglomerations around Valletta as well as the coast ended up being provided with all kinds of defence systems that are mostly still standing.

The British introduced styles of architecture more to their liking, such as the Neo-Classical style and the Neo-Gothic. One can notice some of these buildings in Malta. The latter style was usually much more associated with church buildings, and the magnificent cemetery at Marsa.

The three prehistoric temples of Mnajdra, Qrendi

An 18th -century sketch of the 'Punic Tower', Żurrieq

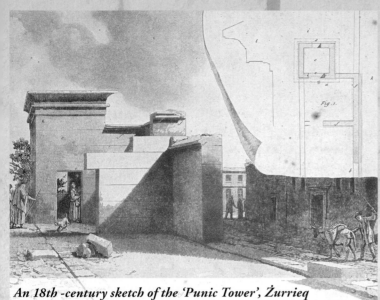

The peristylium with mosaics at the Domus Romana, Rabat

16th-century architecture at the Citadel, Gozo

Auberge of Castile, an 18th-century baroque building, Valletta

The 19th-century Balluta buildings at St Julians

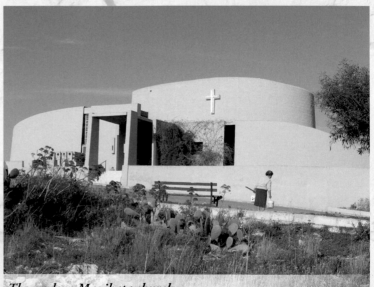

The modern Manikata church

Top and left: The image of the Holy Virgin painted directly on rock is traditionally held to have been painted by St Luke, the apostle who accompanied St Paul on his travels. The painting is still venerated at the cave church in Mellieha.

Top: Votive offerings have been donated to the sanctuary since the middle ages, some of which can be seen in the attached museum.

Right: The modern parish church of Mellieha, dedicated to the Nativity of the Virgin, was built at the end of the 19th century.

Top: Mellieha Bay, one of the most popular sandy beaches of the island.

Left: The film set for the Hollywood film Popeye, in which the famous actor Robin Williams, had starred, is still open to the public.

Mellieħa

The northern part of Malta is characterized by small villages, providing all necessary modern commodities, but surrounded charming countryside views and seascapes that render them so different from the rest of the island's villages. Mellieħa is one of the older villages, although it was practically abandoned for centuries owing to continual piratical raids. The parish church is impressive, but an earlier sanctuary still survives tucked beneath the rocks underneath. Partly carved out into the solid rock, and later on extended, this is the famous Mellieħa Sanctuary which is dedicated to Our Lady in Heaven. This has been one of the most important Marian shrines of Malta for hundreds of years.

The sanctuary is also famous for a painting, executed directly on the rock face, which is traditionally attributed to by St Luke the evangelist, St Paul's companion when they were shipwrecked on the island around 60 AD. Many pilgrimages are held to this church. In the small rooms behind the actual church, there are many votive offerings that testify to the people's belief that Divine help aided them at certain moments in their lives. Survival from shipwrecks, from piratical attacks, dangerous falls, or other incidents are depicted on some of the paintings. There are also contemporary *ex-votoes*, like accidents and medical conditions. The setting of the sanctuary is also very inspiring. Just next to the sanctuary, there is the entrance to Second World War rock-cut shelters which were used during those years of aerial bombardment. These are quite interesting to visit as they offer an opportunity to understand how people managed to stay for long hours, sometimes for days, inside them.

The area around Mellieħa is quite interesting, both in summer and in winter. The countryside offers good walks and beautiful coastal scenery. There are also a couple of places to visit: the seventeenth-century Red Tower, or St Agatha's Tower, overlooking Mellieħa Bay, and Selmun Palace which was built in the eighteenth century, on land owned by a foundation that used its funds to buy the freedom of Christians held as slaves by Muslims.

Mellieħa Bay, Malta's largest sandy beach, is very popular with Maltese and tourists alike. Besides the joy of swimming and participating in sea sport activities, there is also a very interesting small nature reserve, which is open all the year round.

Mellieħa Bay

Mġarr

On the other side of the island, there is another small farming community: the village of Mġarr. Huddled around the main church, with its particular oval shape, the village is much more famous for its prehistoric remains. There include the site at Skorba *[top, next to title: ceramic pot from the Red Skorba Phase found at Mġarr]*, reputedly the earliest village known to have existed in Malta and dating to about 7,000 years ago. This site witnessed many other occupations, ending with the building of two megalithic temples. The other prehistoric site, Ta' Ħaġrat, has got a much more impressive megalithic temple. Both sites are managed by Heritage Malta, and it is advisable to contact the main office if one wishes to visit them. In the vicinity there is a Roman Baths complex which is undergoing restoration.

There are several beautiful mosaic floors, indicating the social status of the family which owned them.

This area has many beautiful bays which provide interesting places for swimming. The most spectacular, for the sea and views, are Ġnejna Bay, Golden Bay, and Għajn Tuffieħa Bay. All three are highly popular and offer also water sports activities. The surrounding countryside is also ideal for rambling, as it also offers impressive coast scenes with high cliffs, various small historical and prehistoric remains, typical farmhouses, and cultivated fields.

This area is also popular for its small restaurants, where the cuisine is good and typical countryside Maltese food is served with abundance and gusto.

The parish church of Mġarr dominates the surrounding fields

Left: The prehistoric temples of Skorba, a site which is important for its discoveries which date back to the earliest man on the island.

Left: The impressive trilithon entrance of Ta Ħaġrat prehistoric temples.

Right: A small limestone architectural model found at Ta' Ħaġtat.

Below: The ruins of the Roman Baths complex, the largest of such complexes discovered in Malta.

Top and right: Paradise Bay is a very popular beach because of its remoteness, seclusion, and clear blue seas and sand.

Top: Armier Bay, relaxing under the palm trees, with a book and with the sea just a few metres away.

Left: Ġnejna Bay offers clear seas and intriguing coastline.

Top: Ghajn Tuffieħa – one of the characteristic bays in the north-west of Malta.

Right: Golden Bay – open beaches and ample space where to relax.

Food in Malta

The history of the Maltese islands has led to a varied cuisine as well. The production of honey in Malta has always been part of the local economy. This is mentioned even during the Roman period, when it is suggested that the name of Malta derived from *mel*, meaning 'honey'. Various classical authors mentioned the good Maltese honey. Honey is still being produced and one highly recommends that a jar or two be taken back home.

Maltese food is, of course, influenced by the Mediterranean diet, although there have been various additions in the last century or two. Rabbit stew is considered one of the great delicacies to be enjoyed while in Malta. Rabbits used to be hunted, but are nowadays reared either in homes or on farms. Nutritionists recommend rabbit meat as a healthy meat.

Eating in Malta is never a complete experience without a visit to a fish restaurant. There are various such places in the islands, a clear indication of their popularity and generally good standards. The fish available depends on the weather as well as the season. Highly recommended are *lampuki*, tuna, octopus, as well as the *ċerna* (grouper) and *denti̇ci* (dentex).

During a visit to a Maltese type of restaurant try to taste the good Maltese bread. Try it spread with olive oil, tomato paste, and sprinkled with olives, capers, and herbs. Make sure to wash it down with some local wine. This is one of the most popular snacks among the Maltese, especially when they are near the sea. You can also add a couple of Maltese *ġbejniet*, small cheeses made from goat's and sheep's milk. There are different types of these cheeses, and all taste excellent.

Sweet delicacies are also varied here in Malta. Nougat can be bought during any religious feast being celebrated in a town or village. There are also 'honey rings' which taste excellent, especially when made with Maltese honey. Yet, for something to have with a tea or coffee, make sure that at one point you will also taste the *pastizzi*. These are made out of pastry, filled either with *ricotta* or peas. They are to be eaten warm.

Maltese wines have recently made great strides forward. Wine has always been a characteristic of the Mediterranean culture. The Maltese wines are very tasty and one can find all kinds of different tastes. A good number of them have received prestigious awards.

Restaurants along Spinola Bay

a. Kappar
b. Zalzett
c. Bigilla
d. Ful
e. Ġbejniet tal-bżar

f. Tadam imqadded
g. Ravjul
h. Ġbejniet friski
i. Żebbuġ
j. Tadam ċatt

k. Bebbux
l. Patata l-forn
m. Galletti
n. Melħ mill-oħxon
o. Ħobż biż-żejt
p. Inbid
q. Ħobża
r. Żejt taż-żebbuġa

A spread of Maltese platters

Qubbajt,
Maltese nougat

Karamelli tal-ħarrub, *boiled sweets*
made from carob syrup.

Ġbejniet friski, *fresh*
goat's cheese

Qassata, *traditional*
sweet Maltese pastry

Qagħqa ta' l-għasel,
honey and treacle ring

Top: Fried rabbit with garlic and herbs is considered to
be Malta's traditional national dish, known as fenkata.

Ħalib bl-għasel, *milk and honey*

Bajtar tax-xewk, *prickly pears*

102

Pastizzi *come with two fillings, cheese (left) and peas (right)*

Timpana, *baked macaroni covered with pastry*

Ħobża, *traditional Maltese bread*

Left: The produce of good quality wine is on the rise in Malta. Below: Kinnie, Malta's bitter sweet soft drink

Top: Fish and seafood sold in the open-air market at Marsaxlokk. In the foreground the dolphin fish (known in Malta as lampuka).

A selection of vegetables grown in Malta

Grape picking

Fishing boats and pleasure yachts lie in anchor at the safe harbour at St Paul's Bay

St Paul's Bay

This bay is so named because, according to tradition, the shipwreck of St Paul around 60 AD occurred on the small islet at the entrance to the bay. In the mid-nineteenth century a massive stone statue of the saint was erected to remind everyone of that particular event. The bay has been highly developed on one side and it is today a very popular tourist area with many hotels, restaurants, and all types of leisure establishments. It is also popular with the Maltese, many of whom now live there all year round while an even larger number of Maltese families have got their summer residences in the area.

The large bay needed to be defended throughout history, and the earliest mention of defence goes back to the medieval times when watch guard duties were organised. Yet, it was during the 17th century that the first permanent tower was erected. This was the Wignacourt Tower, built at the expense of the French Grand Master Alof de Wignacourt. This tower is open for visits throughout the week. Later on other fortifications were erected to complement the defence of this bay.

Due to its distance from Valletta, the area remained sparsely populated and only farmers and fishermen frequented the area. It was only in the second half of the 19th century that the population started to increase, and soon afterwards when public transport became more organised. This led to a number of houses being built, mostly as summer residences. The churches in the village are few in number, although there is one, dedicated to the Shipwreck of St Paul, which traces its history back to the Medieval times. With the continuous increase in population, the village was set up as a separate parish and a larger parish church was build.

From the 1960s onwards the village of St Paul became one of the first zones in Malta that started to be developed as a tourist centre. Hotels, guest houses, restaurants and other tourist establishment were built. Today it is still a highly developed tourist centre. There are various places where one can enjoy swimming along the shore, while in winter times one can easily go on countryside walks in the neighbouring area.

Top: An 18th-century coastal fortification converted into a restaurant.

Right: The massive walls of a 17th-century tower, today housing a museum about military life of the time.

The main pedestrian area of Buġibba

Bugibba and Qawra

One of the bays next to the large one is Salina Bay, so called after the salt pans that were constructed by the knights of St John but which are today not in use. This bay was very important in Roman times, as it went in much deeper into the valley, providing a sheltered harbour. A small community must have lived here as well, as there are several small catacombs in a field near the coast, and other Roman remains in the vicinity. Yet, the earliest human habitation is much older as there has also been discovered at least the remains of two prehistoric temples. One of them, the so-called Bugibba temple is today found within the grounds of one of the leading hotels. It follows the same plan and design of all the other temples, with the difference that one of the stones is carved with fish, thus indicating that fishing was also practiced by the prehistoric communities of Malta. This particular and unique stone *[above; next to title]* is today exhibited at the National Museum of Archaeology in Valletta.

Another interesting archaeological remain that has been discovered in the area are a cluster of early Christian hypogea.

These burial chambers were excavated into the solid rock, and some of them are also highly decorated.

Due to its considerable distance from Mdina and Valletta, this area always needed guard duties to be organized. During the medieval times there was a roster for the males to be present in various areas around Malta in order to offer guard duty. During the 17th century the first of coastal fortifications in the area was built, today being used as a restaurant. Along the same coast, in the 18th century there was erected an entrenchment, which provided the necessary shelter to the soldiers defending the area in case of an attack.

The area nowadays is very popular with Maltese families, as there is ample space where one can have a walk along the shore, while others prefer to spend their day in the adjacent open ground which provides a good place where children can play. Being also close to St Paul's Bay, there are also a number of tourist accommodation establishments, restaurants and other entertainment places.

Top: The inner part of the Salina Bay, with its 16th-century salt pans.

Right: The ruins of the Bugibba prehistoric temple, lying within the grounds of a local hotel

The old parish church of Birkirkara

The Main Villages

Many of the villages of Malta deserve a specific visit. The best time to visit them is during one of their various religious feasts, as that would be the occasion when the village, the parish, and the parishioners would be dressed up in their best livery. Even the churches are best enjoyed during this time.

Birkirkara, the largest urban centre in Malta, traces its origins to medieval times. Today it has grown in several directions but the old core of the village is even more interesting to discover as one needs to pass through the many new streets with buildings to reach it. Next to the main bus terminus there is the old Railway Station which has been turned into a public garden. One can see one of the old carriages and even the station building, with the different class cash points. At the farther end there is the old parish church dedicated to St Mary. This church has been restored and its façade, by local architect Tommaso Dingli, is one of the most beautiful in early seventeenth-century local architecture. The present parish church, dedicated to St Helen, is completely different. It is an 18th-century creation by another Maltese architect,

Domenico Cachia, and it was built in the baroque style. Its internal artistic decorations are a clear indication of the affluence of the people over the years. Attached to this church, there is also a small parish museum. Near it, there are other smaller churches of relevant importance within the local context. One lies just behind the main parish: it is dedicated to Our Lady Tal-Ħerba (of the ruins). Besides the well-decorated interior, there is also a small museum attached to it containing past and recent votive offerings.

Near to Birkirkara there are the so-called **Three Villages** of **Attard**, **Balżan**, and **Lija**. These have become very popular residential areas as can be seen from the increase in their population. Walking along the old centres of the three villages, one gets the impression of a cluster of villas, or countryside *palazzi*, huddling together around a convenient centrally-located church with the small houses coming on later in the day. Some of the *palazzi* have retained some of their past splendour, although because of modern traffic, it is not easy to remember the times when horse-drawn carriages were the order of the day. Follow the streets and be surprised with the various architectural

Attard parish church, built in a Renaissance style

Balzan parish church

A 19th-century garden belveder, Lija

St Philip's parish church, Żebbuġ

gems that come along. The beautifully-decorated façade of the Attard parish church is one of these. Some time should also be reserved for San Anton Gardens, which are part of the Presidential Palace. The original villa was erected as a private residence by the future Grand Master Antoine de Paule. Later on the place was embellished with more gardens and it even became one of the official residences of the grand masters. During the British period, it was used by the British governors and sometimes used by the visiting members of the British royal family. When Malta was declared a republic, the president started to reside here in his official capacity. Today, the palace has retained a lot of its past splendour, although there is nothing missing from the modern comfort.

Żebbuġ is a large village with a considerable population which developed from a cluster of medieval hamlets. The old parts can be easily recognized by the narrow and winding streets, while the newer side has wider roads and larger houses. The stone triumphal arch was erected on the outskirts of the village to commemorate the elevation of the village to a city by Grand Master de Rohan who gave it the title of Città Rohan. Various small churches can be seen in the older part, while the parish church itself is an architectural gem. The village boasts also of widespread popular participation in the Holy Week festivities with a large number of small exhibitions organized by individuals. The three band clubs of the village each organise large displays, making Żebbuġ a big attraction during this period. While walking the streets, notice the various niches adorning the street corners and house façades. One of the popular saints in this village is St Philip, the patron saint, while there are niches showing St Roque, one of the patron saints during the plague.

The large village of **Qormi** has continued to expand in the surrounding fields. Its origins go back to the medieval times, as does that of the parish church of St George. The older part is an authentic medieval labyrinth of streets, alleys, and small openings which render this village an interesting experience. Practically anywhere you go, you are bound to find a bakery. The reason for these many bakeries is that the Order of St John had ordered new bakeries to be established there so that their smoke would control the insects that proliferated in this marshy area. Qormi prides itself on making the best Maltese bread. In the mid-eighteenth century, the village was also given the title of a city, and officially named as Città Pinto, in honour of the grand master who had bestowed this title. Owing to a late cult towards St Sebastian, the patron saint invoked during times of pestilence, a secondary church was built on the outskirts of the village. This area gradually became quite populated and today a newer and a bigger church has been erected in honour of this saint. The new church has got a different architectural style and it dominates the whole area with its large dome and four church belfries.

Żejtun lies very close to Marsaxlokk Bay and this is where the fishermen used to live. Living close to the shore was not a good idea, especially during the summer months when one could end up being taken as a slave. The small village of Żejtun was made up of two distinct districts, one concentrated around the small parish church dedicated to St Catherine of Alexandria, and the other district further inland. Owing to regular piratical attacks, one of the worst being that of 1614 when a good part of the village was devastated, during the seventeenth century it was decided to build a bigger church further inland. The old sixteenth-parish church, with its different style of architecture and interesting features, is still standing and is definitely worth a visit. Żejtun is also a highly interesting village with its small main square dominated by a magnificent baroque church built to the designs of the Maltese architect Lorenzo Gafà, the small narrow and winding streets, the various palatial country houses, and an atmosphere that one can only get by walking its streets. Several archaeological remains have been discovered nearby, one of them being the ruins of a Roman farmhouse, thus attesting to the presence of an agricultural community at least for the last two millennia. Like various village squares in Malta, one tend to find located here or close by the police station and the political party and band clubs. Żejtun was also elevated to the status of a city in the eighteenth century.

Żabbar was originally considered as a small village situated close to the harbour area, mostly inhabited by farmers. Eventually the village attracted more villagers, who settled around one of the most important Marian shrines in the islands dedicated to Our Lady of Graces. Very close to this church is a well-sized church museum with its various exhibits, including a small number of archaeological items which indicate the presence of the earlier inhabitants of the islands. There are also church items, like vestments, liturgical books, altar ornaments, and paintings which used to be inside the church in previous centuries. There is also a small collection of votive offerings, mainly maritime paintings. The village and this sanctuary are quite near the Grand Harbour, where the fleet of the Order had its base.

Gudja is a small village which lies just opposite the modern international airport. Close by to the airport, there is an interesting medieval church, which used to be one of the most important churches on the island and also some prehistoric remains. This church is one historical building that has been restored by Malta's Heritage Trust, *Din L-Art Ħelwa*.

continues on page 114

Qormi parish church dedicated to St George

St Catherine, Żejtun's parish church built by Lorenzo Gafà

Żabbar baroque parish church

Top: Gudja local council and police station.

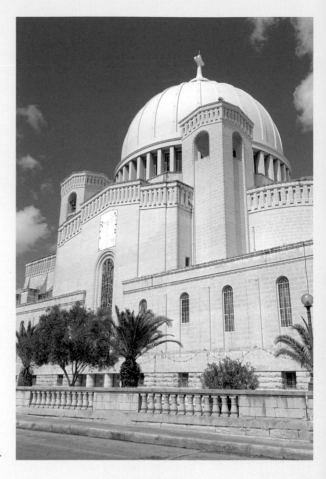

Right: St Sebastian parish church, Qormi built in the 20th century.

Left: San Anton gardens, Attard.

Right: Baking bread in the traditional way in a Qormi bakery.

Left: A sedan chair dating to the 18th-century at Żabbar Sanctuary Museum.

Bottom: Statue of Pope St Gregory the Great close to the old parish church of Żejtun.

continues from page 111

The church is very bare inside, but its architectural features both outside and inside the building are highly interesting. The core of Gudja is interesting, albeit this is a quiet village. The richly-decorated parish church is dedicated to the Assumption of Our Lady. The façade boasts of three bell towers, the only one of its kind in Malta. A third bell tower was added after a foreign resident living in the village donated the money to have it built. On the outskirts of the village, there is an old palatial building, built by a noble family in the eighteenth century, although some structure seems to have always been in the area. This was used as the headquarters by the British naval commanders when they landed in Malta in 1800 to organize the last push towards forcing the besieged French troops of Napoleon to capitulate.

Perched on a high ridge, commanding excellent views of the coastline, as well as the surrounding villages, is **Naxxar**. This village was always well situated as it could easily place guards on these hills to warn of piratical incursions. The area seems to have been occupied since prehistoric times. The fortifications in the area also attest to this importance. A sixteenth-century tower built by a private family was immediately copied with a similar structure erected close by to be used by the captain of the local militia. These two towers are most interesting for those interested in military defences. Close by there are eighteenth- and nineteenth-century fortifications. These are lines of fortifications which follow the natural escarpment

Parish church of St Mary, Gudja

Naxxar parish chruch and main square

114

and were meant to protect the infantry stationed there against an enemy approaching from the coast. One can walk along these fortifications and enjoy outstanding country views. Close by to the two previously-mentioned towers, there is a small country church which is now surrounded by houses. This church is said to have been built near the place where St Paul stopped and preached to the multitude and his words were heard in Gozo. A statue in front of the church shows the saint preaching.

The village has several small churches, besides the parish which is dedicated to Our Lady of Victories. The church is the work of the Maltese architect Tommaso Dingli, with later additions carried out in the following centuries. The interior is fully decorated, like all the major parishes of the islands. Attached there is a small church museum with several old altarpieces, some medieval panels, as well as the whole set of processional statues that are taken around the streets of the village during Good Friday.

Close by to Naxxar, there is **Għargħur** which, till recently was considered just a small village. This has become quite popular in recent years and the increase in population attests to this. The village is surrounded by beautiful countryside, magnificent views of the surrounding coasts and valleys, and some interesting old houses of character. The parish church is another baroque building, with a fine interior, and a magnificent processional statue depicting St Bartholomew.

Għargħur parish church

The lavish interior of Palazzo Parisio, Naxxar

Top: Narrow and shaded village streets offer tranquillity and peace.

Left: Village street corners are usually a popular meeting place, especially when bars are to be found there.

Top: Selling vegetables on a small cart is the best way to reach one's clients in the narrow village streets.

Right: Village squares tend to be the main bus terminus of the locality.

Open air markets are held on different days throughout villages in Malta. One can buy fresh vegetables, fish and other commodities in individual stalls, above, or a collective of stalls, left.

Top: Town houses can have stone statues representing saints placed in niches, as part of the decoration.

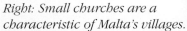
Right: Small churches are a characteristic of Malta's villages.

Top: Closed balconies are so much of the characters of Maltese streets. Some façades are also fancifully decorated, like this house [left] at Għaxaq which is adorned with decorations and letters using seashells stuck into the façade.

Top: Open air cafes and restaurants next to the sea offer the best way to end one's day in a relaxed and pleasant atmosphere.

Right: Town houses are sometimes small museums, with antiques and other collectables adorning all corners.

Festas

Visiting Malta during the summer months is an experience. Yet, this experience will not be taken in full if one does not visit at least one major religious *festa*, the way that only the Maltese know how to do it. The villages vie with each other to make the best outdoor festivities which are planned months ahead. Various fund raising activities are held during the year so that there will always be something to inaugurate the following feast day.

The church is well decked with all its silver, damask curtains, beautiful chandeliers, and all the altars are decorated. Various band marches are held in the village streets, culminating on the last day, when the titular processional statue is taken around the streets carried aloft by enthusiastic parishioners.

In the main square a number of stalls are set up selling various snacks. Highly recommended is the typical nougat, a hard chewy sweet mixed with dried fruit and nuts. There are various types of this sweet, and the stalls selling them are also an attraction in their own right.

All the streets are decorated with flags, drapery, and wooden columns. On top of the columns there are usually statues of other saints or personalities connected with the life of the patron saint. The wooden columns are highly interesting as they are painted to resemble marble. The fireworks are also another important feature as, together with the band clubs, they are the heart of the whole popular celebrations. Besides the churches that are not be missed while visiting the village on its feast day, the various band clubs are also important places to visit, as some of these are located in large palaces, some of which are quite old as well. The exhibited decorations and trophies are a witness to the pride of the band club and its members.

Vittoriosa en fete *for the feast day of its patron saint – St Lawrence*

A big umbrella with decorated drapery at Poala

The decorated interior of Għaxaq parish church

A titular statue against the background of the street decorations

A ground fireworks display in front of the parish church

The illuminated façade of Birkirkara church

The nougat seller

Top: Popular band marches are held in the morning of the eve of the feast, giving a chance for the youngsters and young at heart to celebrate their annual feast day.

Right: Band marches: an essential characteristic of the village festa.

Left: On the evening of the feast day the titular statue is carried solemnly through the main streets of the parish.

Right: Certain parishes are well known for their fireworks displays, which are an attraction to enthusiasts, who flock to the area to appreciate the show.

Left: Other parishes organize horse races in the afternoon along one of the main roads of the town. A traditional horse race held in Victoria, Gozo.

Bottom: Another tradition connected with a religious feast is the regatta held in September in the Grand Harbour.

The Gozo-Malta channel with Comino and its tower in between

The Island of Gozo

Gozo, the second largest island of the Maltese archipelago, is sometimes referred to as the island where time stood still. In certain areas it really looks as if the modern world has still to get there. The fields are still the small family-held units and, generally, the tools used are the traditional ones. It is common to see a farmer going to his field on a mule or a very old and rickety cart. Most of the villages are still small and the narrow and winding streets offer the right atmosphere to make one feel back in time.

The main town is Victoria, or Rabat as it is referred to colloquially. This is a mixture of the old- and the modern new needs in a small community that thrives a lot on tourism, both internal and external. The outskirts of Rabat are full of modern buildings and amenities, but as one gets nearer to the centre, to the small square that doubles up as the main square of the town, if not of the island, one starts to understand the feeling of history. The buildings are mostly either late eighteenth-century or else even nineteenth- and early twentieth-century. Most of these buildings were erected to exploit the available accommodation needed at the time. Today they are still being used almost for the same reason. The square is a hive of activity. The market stalls that can be seen during the morning include hawkers selling different knick knacks, typical vegetable stalls, and fish-sellers. Near the same square one can also buy the odd antique piece of furniture or souvenir. From this square one can either walk towards St George's basilica and the old medieval streetscape, or walk uphill towards the medieval Citadel with its fortifications, cathedral, and magnificent views.

The Citadel is a must for all visitors. The atmosphere of this small fortified place gives an indication of how precarious the islanders' life was in the past. One difficult time was in 1551, when a large piratical force landed in Gozo and, after a three-day siege, killed the only gunner available on the island. They then took almost all the inhabitants off to slavery. The earliest documents that have survived in Gozo date back only to the years after this siege.

The bastions are impressive in their small size. They offer the best views of the surrounding areas, the villages, the hills, and the town of Victoria below it. The Citadel also offers a

The greenery of the fields invites one and all to visit the small island of Gozo

Stone idols discovered at the Xagħra Circle

The imposing façade of the cathedral of Gozo

The interior of Our Lady of Ta' Pinu Sanctuary, Għarb

walk around the streets which have several quaint corners and small museums. There is the Museum of Archaeology with its highly interesting material from prehistory and antiquity; the Folklore Museum; the Natural Science Museum; the Cathedral Museum; and the old small prisons. The cathedral is imposing, with its flight of steps and the seventeenth-century baroque façade. It was designed by Lorenzo Gafà, the Maltese architect who was responsible for the cathedral in Malta and many other churches. The interior of the cathedral is decorated with the usual side altars, paintings, statues, and an eye-catching false dome painting by an Italian eighteenth century painter.

The other side of Rabat, towards St George's basilica, also deserves a visit, with its narrow streets, particular architectural features, the actual church itself, and its small open spaces. From this town it is possible to visit all the other places of interest in Gozo, as the main bus terminus is to be found here. The other small villages and the sites in certain outlying districts should also not to be missed. Gozo can easily be visited, very hurriedly, in a day, but one should spend more than just a couple of days here, as there is much more than one would expect.

A village that cannot be missed because of its various historical and architectural remains is Xagħra. The prehistoric temples of Ġgantija are the oldest free-standing building in the world and UNESCO World Heritage site. The complex is impressive even though it lies in ruins. Nearby there is a small windmill, which has been restored and houses a folklore museum. To the other side of the Xagħra high ground, there is the famous Calypso Cave, which is connected with the legend of Ulysses who was kept here for seven years by the nymph Calypso, before she was allowed to return back to his ever-suffering wife, Penelope. The view from this point, above the entrance to a small cave, is fantastic. The sandy bay itself is also rich in archaeological material. There are the remains of Roman Baths still preserved beneath the sand dunes. There are then fortifications which mostly date to the eighteenth century, one of which is actually a wall which was erected at the bottom of the sea to deter invaders. The long black line across the bay is what remains of this submerged wall.

Ta' Pinu basilica is another place not to be missed. This is one of the few churches of the islands which has developed beyond territorial parochialism. It is visited by one and all, and prayers are said inside this church usually to ask for some help, or to offer thanks to Our Lady for help already given. A visit inside this sanctuary attests to this great devotion. The architecture is unique, especially the stonework, and one should notice the many votive offerings offered to Our Lady as a sign of thanksgiving over the centuries. All the side altars have got mosaics instead of titular paintings; the only one painted on canvas is the original painting of the small church. This great devotion originated after a spinster, who used to stop to say a prayer before returning back home after a day's work in the fields, recounted a number of experiences when Our Lady spoke to her. This led to official recognition by the Church and pilgrimages being organized by the population. This church falls within the limits of the parish of Għarb, and countryside walks in the vicinity, as well as a visit to the village square of Għarb, are also recommended. The façade of this parish church is quite unusual. Also worth a visit is the small private Folklore Museum.

Dwejra is a natural site which attracts a good number of visitors for various reasons. The views are spectacular, the sea is always inviting, and the walking is exhilarating. Here there is the unique Inland Sea, and one can easily take a small boat ride out of the natural tunnel entrance into the open seas. There is the Azure Window with its deep blue sea, and the almost continuous presence of divers in and around it. Walking in this area is also recommended, especially in the cooler months. To the other side of the Inland Sea, there is another small secluded bay with its impressive rock offering protection to any vessel that takes shelter inside it. Access to this rock – Fungus Rock – is restricted as it has been declared a nature reserve. During the eighteenth century, it was also protected by the state, as it was thought that a particular plant that was thought could only be found there, held excellent medicinal values. Therefore the grand masters protected the plant and the rock. Although today we know that this plant grows elsewhere, the natural habitat of the rock is considered to be of the great utmost importance and has been given legal protection.

The small seventeenth-century coastal watch tower, the small church dedicated to St Anne, and the variety of small buildings that are to be found in and around this area, makes this place an idyllic stop. On the bare Globigerina limestone, one can also trace the enigmatic cart-ruts, those remains which still solicit mystery and debates about their date and use. Walking along the shore, one can notice a multitude of fossils which are part of the natural history of the islands. Their study gives clear indications of how the islands were formed and through which processes they passed. Picking fossils is prohibited by law.

Nadur is another large village. Its parish church dominates the skyline and the village square. The small bays to be found in its vicinity are very popular with locals and the few tourists who manage to find them. The countryside walks also offer relaxing moments, as from here one can easily reach the coast or other nearby villages. A walk to the Kennuna Tower area offers an excellent view of the area and the channel between the islands. From here one can easily observe the traffic in the channel, as well as the popular Blue Lagoon in Comino.

continues on page 130

A Roman oscillum *on display at the Museum of Archaeology*

The typical main square of Għarb

The geological formation of the Inland Sea

Top: The medieval fortifications of the Citadel blend well with the later walls.

Right: The main corridor of of Ġgantija North prehistoric temple, providing also an idea of the type of stones used for the building of the oldest free standing building in the world.

Left: Calypso kept Odysseus for seven years with her according to the Homeric epic. Traditionally their home was the greenery of the fields, the beauty of the sea, and the sandy beaches of Ramla Bay.

Right: The small and busy harbour of Mġarr, which controls all the sea traffic between the two main islands.

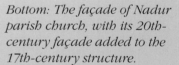

Left: The modern large parish church of Xewkija boasts of an impressive interior with one of the biggest domes in the world.

Bottom: The façade of Nadur parish church, with its 20th-century façade added to the 17th-century structure.

Left: Strolling along the coast provides pleasure, especially near the Fungus Rock at Dwejra, where it was thought that it was the only place where a particular medicinal root plant grows. Access to the rock is prohibited.

Right: The Azure Window at Dwejra, a favourite place for photos and for diving enthusiasts. The Blue Hole in front of it provides excellent underwater scenery.

Top: The recently-developed Xlendi Bay is very popular with holiday makers and boat owners.

Left: Typical terraced and small fields worked with modern tools

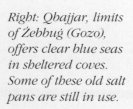

Top: Revellers enjoying the band marches during the feast day of St George, in Victoria, Gozo.

Right: Qbajjar, limits of Żebbuġ (Gozo), offers clear blue seas in sheltered coves. Some of these old salt pans are still in use.

continues from page 125

Also easily visible from this high place is Xewkija, with its great parish church dome dominating not only the village but also the surrounding countryside. The village was long considered as a risk, because it was usually amongst the first to be attacked by corsairs. For this reason a number of small watch towers were built on its outskirts, one of which is still standing. This particular tower lies next to the road that leads to the small heliport that provides air connection between the islands.

The parish church of Xewkija is a marvel to see. The sheer size for the small village, the sculpture and decorations inside, and the view from the rooftop are remarkable. Yet, another plus point is that the old church, which was a small but highly-interesting baroque church, was not completely demolished. The altars were dismantled and rebuilt in a semblance of order next to the main church. Today visitors can see the sculptures of the old church and its various paintings and other decorations.

Gozo is a place to enjoy life at a slower pace. The various small villages, and the sheer small size and short distances offer the opportunity to see much of the island. Various walks can be enjoyed, offering a dose of everything – countryside views, coastal scenery, small farmhouses and churches, legends, and hard-working farmers.

There are a number of bays for relaxing and swimming in the clear blue sea. Some bays are rather difficult to get to, but most have got good signs and are not as crowded as the bays in Malta. The most popular is Ramla Bay, with its marvellous red, soft sand, which can be very hot for walking upon barefoot. Two excellent small fishing villages should be visited, namely Marsalforn and Xlendi, while Mġarr, down at the harbour also offers some good food. On such a small island as Gozo, surrounded by sea and the presence of fishermen, it stands to reason that there are a good number of fish restaurants, many of which offer good value for money. The busy Marsalforn Bay area with its various restaurants offers a good place for an evening stroll. Xlendi also has its scenic valley view and several restaurants actually placed on the edge of the sea shore.

The wide open bay of Marsalforn, very popular with locals and tourists alike

A Gozo bus with its typical colour scheme in front of San Lawrenz parish church

Comino tower which was built in 1618 to provide protection to those crossing between the islands

Comino

Lying between the two larger islands of Malta and Gozo, and usually seen only while crossing between them, Comino is renowned for its natural state and the clear blue seas that surround it. It is a very popular place with the Maltese and tourists alike, especially during the summer months.

The island is practically uninhabited, except for a family of farmers who still maintain their own farm and take care of their fields there. They have the luxury of a small church which, in summer time, is always full with holidaymakers trying to squeeze inside. This church dates back to medieval times and retains architectural features as well as internal furnishings which are unique to the islands.

The tower was built in 1618 by Grand Master Alof de Wignacourt who provided it with the necessary funds and artillery pieces out of his own pocket. This tower was built to offer better protection to all those who wanted to make the crossing between the islands. Today, the tower is still retained by the Armed Forces of Malta for observation purposes. The large building close to it was built as a hospital by the British. Facing Malta, there is a recently-restored coastal battery, which was built to offer better firing power against naval raiders.

The most impressive area of Comino is the Blue Lagoon. Protected by the small islet of Cominotto, the waters here are usually calm and safe to swim. The sea is deep, even though it does not give that impression; yet, it is safe enough for one to swim. Good swimmers can cross to the smaller islet without any problems. One can reach Comino either by getting the small ferries that operate near the Gozo Ferry terminals in both Malta and Gozo, or on one of the various day trips organized by various companies. For those who would really prefer a relaxing and a quiet holiday, one can also contemplate on having a break at the hotel, the only one on the island which is a nature reserve. Besides the Blue Lagoon, there are other nice rocky beaches that can be visited, and swimming is also possible at certain places.

The clear blue seas and the famous Blue Lagoon of Comino

Top: Scuba diving is a popular sport with diving enthusiasts as the blue seas of Comino provide spectacular views all around.

Right: A walk along the coast of Comino will provide one with interesting terrain and scenic views.

Left: Relaxing on the sun bed, inside a natural cave, with the open seas in front of you ... a typical Maltese summer day.

Right: Perched on the high cliffs of Comino, the Sta Maria Tower still provides the necessary protection to the boats that sail in between the islands.

Left:The interior of the medieval and only church on Comino is interesting and unique. Its architecture and its wooden screen make this church important to local architectural history.

Bottom: An aerial view of Comino provides a better idea of its location with regards to the main islands.

135

Buskett to Għar il-Kbir and Dingli

One can reach Buskett Gardens by taking either Bus Nº 80 or Nº 81. The first stops at Rabat, while the second goes on to Dingli. Preferably one should start the walk from the bus terminus of Rabat, as there are several interesting places along the route.

Follow the signs to Buskett and pay attention as the street is a busy one. Amongst the first details to notice is an archaeological site, which lies between a petrol station and the old medieval Santa Spirito Hospital. The site has provided archaeologists with material dating from pre-Roman times. The old hospital building, which was the only one in Malta before the arrival of the Order of St John, was still in use till the 1960s. Today it houses the National Archives, mainly those dating from the British period onwards. The first church and convent of the Dominican Order was established here in Rabat and today is still a major Marian site. The next important site on this walk is the Presidential Palace, the former summer residence of the grand masters and the British governors. Verdala Palace was designed by Gerolamo Cassar in the sixteenth century. It was embellished during the eighteenth century and it has retained its aura of a princely home. Its interior is richly decorated with paintings and period furniture. The view from the rooftop is magnificent. There is also a small church within the grounds of the palace which is still in use.

Along the walk one can easily understand why the grand masters wanted to have their country residence situated here, away from the worries of the government, as well as near the Buskett Gardens where they could practise their favourite pastime, hunting. This small wood is still the centre of activity especially during the national feast day of SS Peter and Paul, or the *Imnarja* as the Maltese refer to it. On that day an agricultural show is held in the gardens, while on the eve of

The impressive Verdala Palace at Buskett Gardens

29 June, the feast day, there is a lot of evening activity with families and friends meeting up to eat rabbit, drink wine, and sing as our forefathers used to do.

The Clapham Junction cart ruts area is quite interesting. There is a unique series of cart ruts, which have already been mentioned in the section about archaeology. Here there are quite a lot of them, and their concentration has given rise to the nickname of Clapham Junction, indicating that the whole system looks like the busy London railway station. Nearby there are Roman quarries and various Punic rock-cut tombs. Close by there is the largest cave complex which is known to have been used as a habitation at least till the early nineteenth century. Various documents attest that the community here was quite happy with its own lifestyle, and they always referred to themselves as inhabitants of Għar il-Kbir, 'the Large Cave'. In the nineteenth century, the British authorities fearing that an epidemic might erupt because of the unhygienic living conditions of this community, forcefully evicted the inhabitants and partly destroyed the roof so that they would not return.

Walking towards Dingli Cliffs, one comes atop the highest ridge in Malta, with a view taking in the high cliffs of the area, as well as the small islet of Filfla. Walking towards the village of Dingli and take the bus back to Valletta.

The Medieval Santo Spirito Hospital, Rabat

The enigmatic and controversial cart-ruts

Silence and space at the Dominican cloister

Medieval cave dwellings of Għar il-Kbir

Mġarr to Mellieħa

S tart the walk from the main square of Mġarr, which can be reached by taking bus Nº 47 from Valletta. The major feature of this village is the main parish church, with its oval dome, dominating the skyline and the countryside. There are two important prehistoric sites within the limits of the village, both of which can be visited: Skorba temples which include the remains of the earliest village in Malta and Ta` Ħaġrat temples nearer the main square.

Walk towards Ġnejna Bay, passing by a building which is known as Zamitello Palace. A legend connected with this palace says that the daughter of its owner escaped from home as she did not want to marry an old Sicilian nobleman. One can either walk down the hill towards Ġnejna Bay, and then find a way up along the side of the hill towards the seventeenth-century coastal watch tower, or else take the road on the right-hand side, and keep on walking until the tower comes in view. Walking towards this tower, stop and admire the view and the strategic positions of these towers. Walking along the edge of the hill and reach a place from where to look down onto another bay,

Għajn Tuffieħa. Walking down towards the bay can be tricky but not difficult. The flat-topped hill that separates the two bays was actually a Bronze Age site where a village was established, sometime around 2000 BC. This bay was also known as Military Bay, as it was used by the British army to train its soldiers. Note the delicate flora and fauna. The clay cliffs provide the necessary water and therefore a little bit of green that can be noticed here. The other bay is known as Golden Bay, another popular bay with Maltese and tourists alike. These three bays are in fact very popular and very much frequented in summer.

Take the path from behind the Radisson hotel, and enjoy a highly invigorating walk, with splendid views, the sea breeze, and the open countryside. This walk leads to Anchor Bay where there is the set used for the filming of *Popeye*, starring Robin Williams. A short walk will take you towards Għadira, or Mellieħa Bay. If you feel like some more walking, you can visit the Għadira Nature reserve, or else a walk up towards the Red Tower. There are buses to Valletta from the Mellieħa Bay terminus.

The parish church of the Assumption, Mġarr

Top: The trilithon entrance to Ta' Ħaġrat prehistoric temples.

Right: Aerial photo of the Skorba archaeological area, an important prehistoric site.

Top: The boathouses at Ġnejna Bay during summer.

Left: Palazzo Zamitello – a quaint country residence.

Top: Għajn Tuffieħa – beach and landscape.

Right: The nature reserve at Mellieħa Bay.

Siġġiewi to Wied iż-Żurrieq

Take bus Nº 89, and stop in the main square of Siġġiewi. Follow the directions to the Limestone Heritage and one can easily start one's walk with a visit to this highly interesting place. This old disused quarry which has been turned into a touristic and an educational experience. Walk into the quarry and follow the history of quarrying as well as being able to look inside a quarry. There is a small museum with old tools of the trade. Return back to the main road and follow the signs towards Wied iż-Żurrieq.

The road is somewhat busy, although the walk is through country roads. Just outside the village limits there is a small church, which is still a dominating piece of architecture. Dedicated to Our Lady of Providence, it was built in the eighteenth century, with the portico being added when the building started to subsidise. Owing to the presence of this church the whole area is referred to as 'of the Providence'. The same name was taken on by a very commendable institution, the House of Providence, a cluster of buildings which had started as a very small organisation to house people with special needs, especially those whom their families could not keep at home. This institution, although set up by a priest, is a charitable institution and it survives only through public generosity. Thus, the name of the House of Providence is very apt.

The area is surrounded by fertile fields and the stone is also good for quarrying. One can take the road leading down towards Għar Lapsi, one of the few coves on this side of the island. It is also used by fishermen who keep their boats and fishing tackle in small rooms excavated into the rock.

The adventurous can walk along the shore, and will arrive just below the Mnajdra prehistoric temples. Otherwise one can return to the top of the road and walk towards the Ħaġar Qim and Mnajdra area. A stop here is highly recommended, especially for those interested in prehistory. To reach Wied iż-Żurrieq, walk along the main road which will lead you to the top of the road that leads down towards this interesting inlet. This is a very busy small quay, especially in the morning, when tourists take boat rides to the Blue Grotto and the other small caves of the area. From here one can either walk towards the village of Żurrieq to take a bus to Valletta, or else wait for a bus which comes down to this area, although rather irregularly.

A quiet moment in the main square of Siġġiewi

Limestone Heritage – an experience in a quarry

Our Lady of Providence, Siġġiewi

The Ħaġar Qim Temples

Boat rides to the Blue Grotto

Fishermen at Għar Lapsi

Victoria to l'Għadira ta' San Rafflu

There are many places where one can organize a walk in Gozo. This walk is not a difficult one, and it will lead you also through some interesting places. Start from the centre of Victoria and take the road to the small hamlets of Kerċem and Sta Luċija. Just before entering Kerċem, make sure that you leave the main road and go towards the small Lunżjata valley, an oasis of peace throughout the year. It used to be part of an ecclesiastical benefice, and, because of the abundance of water, it was considered as a rich one. A small church abuts the cliff wall. The church is dedicated to the Annunciation, hence the name of the valley, is well looked after and used by the local people and farmers. In spite of its size, the church caters for the main religious functions. Farther down the valley, notice the water flowing beneath a small stone bridge across the valley. Indeed the fields here never lack crops. The path stops in front of a public water fountain, with its fresh water coming out from rock-cut channels, providing a fresh respite, especially during the hot summer months.

Walk towards the parish church of Kerċem, a small but richly decorated church, which you can visit if it is open. Take the road to the side of the church which will lead one to the end of your walk. The signs indicate Sarraflu or San Rafflu. The views from this high point are marvellous. This is the best place to have a view of Xlendi Bay from a completely different angle.

At the end of this walk, one reaches a small fresh-water pond, surrounded by lush vegetation and usually with some water-fowl and fresh-water fish inside. At the turning of this road, one can take the left-hand side, which is a country lane that leads to the fields. Follow this passage for about 30 minutes, which will take you the edge of the cliff. Notice the remains of a Punic sanctuary, and one of the most fantastic views in Gozo, looking down on the Dwejra and Fungus Rock area. This is a walk where one needs to be prepared for heights, and pay attention not to walk too close to the edge. Otherwise it is a very interesting walk.

The rugged coastline near Xlendi

Top: The small parish church at Kerċem.

Right: The Annunciation church next to the lavish valley of Lunżjata.

Top: Dwejra and the Fungus Rock area seen from Wardija heights.

Left: The Għadira (pond) ta' San Rafflu (Sarraflu) limits of Kerċem.

Bottom: The Punic sanctuary on the cliff edge of Wardija.

MALTA
History & Tradition

2008 Edition

First published in Malta in 2007

by Book Distributors (BDL) Limited

Produced in collaboration with Promotion Services Ltd.

ISBN English editions:

978-99909-72-81-8 (paperback)

978-99909-72-82-5 (hardback)

Author: Vincent Zammit

Photography & Book Design: © 2007 Daniel Cilia

Main photography done with Fuji FinePix S2, S3, S5 Pro cameras

War photos on page 3, 26 and 27 from Wikipedia Commons

Independence and Republic Day photos DOI, Malta

Printed and bound by Gutenberg Press Ltd